Quest *for* Love

True Stories of Passion and Purity

Elisabeth Elliot

Fleming H. Revell
A Division of Baker Book House Co
Grand Rapids, Michigan 49516

© 1996 by Elisabeth Elliot Gren

Published by Fleming H. Revell
a division of Baker Book House Company
P.O. Box 6287, Grand Rapids, MI 49516-6287

New paperback edition published in 2002

Printed in the United States of America

Library of Congress Cataloging-in-Publication Data

Elliot, Elisabeth.
    Quest for love / Elisabeth Elliot.
      p.   cm.
    ISBN 0-8007-5821-8 (paper)
    1. Love—Religious aspects—Christianity. 2. Courtship—
Religious aspects—Christianity. 3. Marriage—Religious aspects—
Christianity. I. Title.
    BV4639.E45   1996
    248.4—dc20   96-6791

For current information about all releases from Baker Book House, visit our web site:
                    http://www.bakerbooks.com

Ask the former generations
  and find out what their fathers learned,
for we were born only yesterday and know nothing,
  and our days on earth are but a shadow.
Will they not instruct you and tell you?
  Will they not bring forth words from their under-
    standing?
Can papyrus grow tall where there is no marsh?
  Can reeds thrive without water?
While still growing and uncut,
  they wither more quickly than grass.
Such is the destiny of all who forget God;
  so perishes the hope of the godless.
What he trusts in is fragile;
  what he relies on is a spider's web.

Job 8:8–14

Let us be Christ's men from head to foot, and give no
chances to the flesh to have its fling.

Romans 13:14 *Phillips*

Quest *for* Love

Contents

Acknowledgments

My sincere thanks to all those correspondents who allowed me to use excerpts from their letters. Some names have been changed.

Special thanks to Tom Griffith, Ivy George, Frank Murray, John Mallon, John Vanderhorst, and Diane Poythress for the use of their published writings.

I am grateful to Mrs. Fred Malir for her husband's story; to Jan Winebrenner, author of *Steel in His Soul;* and Overseas Crusades for Dick Hillis's story; to Courtney Anderson for excerpts from *To the Golden Shore,* the Adoniram Judson story; to John C. Pollock for excerpts from *Hudson Taylor and Maria.*

Introduction

The universal quest for love has always had its difficulties. At present it seems to have become a minefield—a very dangerous place through which, in order to thread one's way safely, one needs a guide who is thoroughly acquainted with the course.

This is mostly a book of stories, stories about how men and women find each other. Some of them, following the best of all guides, did it wisely. Others did not. I hope my readers will discern which examples are worth following.

To marry or not to marry is first of all, gentlemen, an issue for *you*. Most of us women would like to have a husband, and quite a few of us believe that men should do the wooing. We may be as educated, as smart, as capable of making big money as you are, but we were not created to be competitors, and we really don't want to do the hunting. We want you to do it.

But how? Many are the ways in which a man has won a maiden, but the wisest man who ever lived confessed that this was a matter too amazing for him. If it stumped Solomon (who, be it remembered, had three hundred mistresses and seven hundred wives), what chance has an honest young man today amid the myriad causes of confusion that Solomon never had to contend with?

For our blessing and joy God ordained marriage. It follows, then, that Satan opposes it—craftily, powerfully, hatefully.

People take their cues from stories, but movies and television have destroyed *context*, the associated surroundings within which stories are understood. The meaning of home, fireside, the loyal lifetime love of a man and a woman, the security of a father's lap—the dependable context in which love used to be learned—is gone. How much extramarital sexual activity goes on because the media portray it as far more exciting than marital love?

During the Vietnam war, tradition was questioned, ridiculed, and finally trashed. What parents had taught no longer carried any weight. The Baby Boomers (those born between 1946 and 1964) stumbled into new territory. Tradition and custom, which have endured because they *work,* became pejoratives—restrictive, irrelevant, uninteresting. What mattered was to do one's own thing, and there were no directives for that.

One Baby Boomer wrote to me, "I was in high school from '68–'72. The world turned upside down. The sexual revolution took full swing, my schoolgirl fantasies of love and romance died a slow and painful death. Courting and respect disappeared. Dating became a battleground, virtue a hindrance instead of a ticket of entitlement. To maintain high moral standards in this world spells a lot of rejection for a woman nowadays. I have prayed for a Christian man with high ideals but never found one. The majority of men in our society do not believe in moral ethics or virginity. Mother always told me men were gentlemen in the majority, and didn't pressure nice girls. Wish I'd been born in that era! To do what is right is a timeless truth."

Feminist doctrine has caused bewilderment about the true meaning of masculinity and femininity. We were told that the difference between the sexes was a mere anatomical triviality that had nothing to do with our respective places in society, the workplace, the church, or the home. We believed the lie about equality and interchangeability. As women learned self-assertion and aggressiveness, men learned to feel guilty about being men, and began to back off. Those whom God created to be initiators, protectors, and providers no longer understood their assignment, and women wondered why they were not being sought.

A woman lawyer from New York City wrote, "The church is plagued with weak men and strong women (the latter in much larger numbers). It seems that men have become effeminate (some to the point of becoming gay) and women have become overly aggressive, both personally and professionally (myself not exempted).

"The more aggressive 'masculine' men (to whom I find myself attracted) are usually non-Christians. Christian men are afraid of commitment, unduly uptight about their sexuality, afraid to express interest."

As you read the letters and stories that follow, study the revelations of the hearts of men and women. Do they not cause you to tremble at the thought of trifling with such? I found myself turning constantly to God, beseeching His help for my helplessness, asking His wisdom.

Moral blindness and stupidity result from an unwillingness to learn from the experience of elders. "When venturing into new territory," wrote Lance Morrow, "where mere habit will no longer suffice, people require the stabilizing, consoling, instructing influence of other human tales."

The truth of that statement was brought strongly home to me at a student convention in Kansas City. When my turn came to speak I was not surprised to see skepticism on some of those bright young faces. What could this old woman possibly have to say to people young enough to be her grandchildren? My talk was entitled "The Path of Endurance." It was about, of all things, sexual restraint.

They listened—very quietly—because I told them a story. It was the love story of two college students who, though wildly and helplessly in love, endured. They managed to keep their clothes on and stay out of bed until their wedding night five years later. I urged my audience to guard the priceless and irreplaceable gift of virginity with which each of us is born, to keep it intact for the right person, not to squander it on the wrong one. That's the way it was meant to be. Abstinence greatly enhances the pleasure that the Creator of sex had in mind.

The response was astounding. Total silence while I spoke. Eyes glued to the speaker. You would have thought I had discovered something original.

When I finished there was not only applause. They leaped to their feet. They stamped. They whooped, whistled, and cheered for what seemed a long time.

What did this mean? I believe it substantiates my deep conviction that in every generation there are those who not only hunger for the truth, but also search desperately for a high, even an "impossibly" high, standard. What standards have been held before them for the past few decades? They have watched the movies, the videos, the TV dramas. They have read the romance and adventure novels. They have drunk in the messages, "Everybody's doing it," "You're not a man till you've slept with a woman," "You have a right to your own body," "Use it or lose it," and "Who can tell you what's right for *you?* Do what feels good! Don't let anybody jam their morality down your throat!"

Those students heard a different story and on that same day bought six thousand copies of a book called *Passion and Purity.* Many of them already knew too much about passion but had hardly heard of purity.

A man named Scott wrote to me, "My life will never be the same after that bitter cold December evening in Kansas City when I sat in the Civic Auditorium and heard the words that changed my life forever. Tears streamed down my face. I realized my life would never be the same. I know my marriage will be enriched by my abstinence until that special night."

I began to get letters not only from high school and college students, but also from readers of all ages, letters that described crazily destructive ways of going about finding that elusive thing called romance, or, more often nowadays, "relationship." I learned of woeful misconceptions regarding masculinity and femininity, story after story of the calamitous results of the dating game. Many bewailed what they called the "loss" of their virginity, forgetting that they had chosen to give it away. When what had been called repressions and taboos were lightly discarded, that wonderful sexual "freedom" that had held such promise generated unimagined misery. College physicians found themselves treating male students for *impotence*, for when you look for satisfaction in many beds you find it in none.

There was also a surprising number of letters breathing a sigh of relief that someone else in the world believed what the letters' authors believed about purity.

"I agonized through *Passion and Purity*, hating it and loving it. You tell it as God expects it, and it hurts a lot."

"I've decided I won't date any guy until he reads it and tells me he agrees with it!"

"If I ever have a serious girlfriend she'll read P & P."

"It introduced *faith*, a foreign concept to most of my age group."

Of course I challenged the girl who told me she'd read the book two hundred times: "You don't really expect me to believe that, do you?"

"Honestly, Mrs. Elliot, *two hundred times!*"

One girl said that when she reads *Passion and Purity* on the subway she finds people craning their necks to read over her shoulder.

People told me how difficult it was to stand alone among their peers. An officer who had been in the army for eight years recounted ingenious schemes women had tried in order to rob him of his virginity.

A twenty-two-year-old man wrote, "I've read P & P (one of my all-time favorites) about seven times. Practical, roll-up-your-sleeves Christianity, too often lacking among Christians of my generation. We've had our ears tickled and we are tired of it. We make P & P required reading for all incoming freshmen men in our Christian group at Harvard."

"Why hasn't somebody told us this stuff?" was a question that became a motif in those letters. Why had they not heard it, as I had, from parents, teachers, preachers, college professors? Why had they not had access to the stories of those who had waited, endured, and found the joy of self-denial?

That book had nothing new, nothing innovative, nothing original to say. The story was my own, of course, but the principles were not of my own devising. Were they Victorian? No. Much older. The story was simply the vehicle for some timeless truths that had been articulated over and over, far more effectively than I was able to do. The trouble was these young men and women had been carried away by tales in which self-indulgence and uncontrolled passion were presented as the highway to happiness and fulfillment. Their heroes were athletes and entertainers who regarded sex as a game, the body of one of the opposite sex as a toy, and who boasted of sexual promiscuity as though it were a laudable achievement, even a virtue.

Those letters set me to mulling over this dangerous game called dating. When we were college students Jim Elliot had once bought me a Coke and once invited me to accompany him to a missionary meeting. That was as close as we came to dating. No danger there. It is heartening to hear from men and women who perceive the fallacies of that game, have made up their minds to enhance their passions by preserving their purity, and have chosen the path of obedience. Read the excerpts from biographies of a few decades or a century ago, when dating was unheard of. Read the letters from contemporaries, stories of a faithful Shepherd's bringing two people together. No two stories are alike, for He knows His sheep, calls them by name, and leads them in paths of righteousness.

I leave it to the reader to discern the better way.

I hope the Scriptures that head each chapter will help toward this discernment. Some individuals or groups may find further help in the reflections that follow the chapters.

1

A Matter of Timing

I trust in You, O LORD;
I say, "You are my God."
My times are in your hands.

Psalm 31:14–15

"I married late, at thirty-three. This was approximately twelve years after the time I first wanted to get married. Twelve years doesn't seem so long now, but then it seemed an eternity.

"For about half of those twelve years, I tried the world's way of getting married. Not being a Christian, I assumed the burden of finding a wife was entirely my own. I never had the stomach for singles' bars and computer match-ups and that sort of thing, but I was ever the eagle-eyed hunter. Whatever business each day involved, a part of my attention was always given to the hunt. Was this the day? Was she the one? Should I have started a conversation? Should I have pressed her for a date?

"This approach created much anxiety and regret. I was haunted by the thought of missed opportunities, or of not having exerted myself enough. Even when an acquaintanceship got going, it gave little satisfaction, since I could tell pretty soon that it wouldn't lead to marriage. What it did often lead to was emotional entanglements, false hopes, and bruised hearts.

"By twenty-six I was getting nervous as one after another of my friends got married and started families. Then various providences brought me to Massachusetts, where I became a Christian and was baptized.

"When the church's view of courtship and marriage was explained to me, I was flabbergasted. What? Stop hunting, stop dating, just leave it to God and *pray?* And go through a *minister?* Accustomed as I was to going after what I wanted, this seemed almost a cop-out; it was too passive, practically un-American. Yet it also had an appeal, especially as I observed the happy families of those who had gone that route. There seemed to be some proof in the pudding, and I ventured to try it.

"At first it brought a marvelous sense of relief. For the first time in years I relaxed, letting go and letting God. I fully believed that He wishes to grant us the desires of our heart. I'd waited this long; I could wait a little longer for the perfect wife God had in store for me.

"Then, as lonely weekend followed lonely weekend, my resolve began to weaken. I had a good job and a new circle of Christian friends. I even lived with a godly couple who tried to disciple me. But the 'old man' in me began to kick at the new constraints. After all, didn't God help those who helped themselves? Wasn't this waiting for Heaven's choice a little extreme?

"The upshot was that I decided to cheat. I went through the cycle one more time, till conscience gnawed and my relation to God withered. I finally broke free after a timely warning from a minister. Then, leaving behind more hurt feelings, I moved closer to fellowship with the church people, for my own protection.

"Subsequent years were spiritually rich and emotionally rocky. By thirty-two, being single had become my quiet obsession. I didn't discuss it much but had begun wondering if God wanted me never to marry. The prospect tormented me. I recognized that many single people seemed fulfilled and happy, that Scripture endorsed either condition and even seemed to give an edge to singleness, that great works of faith had been accomplished by the unmarried, not least by Jesus Himself.

"But still, I wanted to get married. If lifelong bachelorhood was to be my cross I wasn't sure I could bear it. Each passing year deepened the sense of isolation, of deficiency, of not fitting in. I found myself half wishing I were a Catholic; at least those in religious life who never married got some spiritual 'credit.' But to be Protestant and single just meant feeling left out.

"Even as anxiety deepened, God planted a name in my ear. It was of someone who, on the face of it, seemed highly unsuitable. The gaps of age, background, experience were too great. Yet the thought wouldn't go away.

"God had acted likewise with the young lady. It finally came out, and we were swept together in what felt like an arranged marriage—arranged by God. I never sensed His will so clearly. And His choice was vindicated by a union so blissful that a description of it would sound gloating.

"For me, the most striking lesson of it was the superiority of God's timing to mine. My wife, revealed daily as an ideal partner, is twelve years younger. At the time I felt ready to marry, she was in the fourth grade. It wouldn't have done, and so I had to wait.

"Of course I didn't know that at the time. Like Job, I saw only my own immediate woes. Lacking God's perspective, I kicked against the pricks. We're told to trust, given examples of His faithfulness in both Scripture and our own lives, and yet how easily we forget and begin to doubt Him!

"My advice to singles who want to marry is: hang on. Don't despair of God's resources, so infinitely greater than ours. Don't limit His capacity to bring a mate out of nowhere, when the pool of candidates seems small and hopeless. Don't chafe at Scripture's stress on waiting to know God's will in the matter. He has a will for you, whether you follow it or not. When you get ahead of God and try to force things, the consequences are often tragic. The statistics tell the tale; so do the personal cases we all hear of misfired romances and wretched marriages.

"The way of courtship I learned in our church, as unusual as it seems in these times, appears to me to be God's answer to today's confusion. Those who grew up understanding these things do not always appreciate them, and often take sound and happy marriages for granted. They may hanker for a more 'normal' approach, whereas those of us who have tried 'normality' can testify to its inadequacy.

"In the end, of course, none of us can assure the happiness of anyone else. Nor can we just glibly urge patience on single people, since it may not be God's will for them to marry. But we can comfort one another and give mutual encouragement in the acceptance of that will. Whether we're single or married, life will bring sorrows, but our touchstone of joy remains the steady bearing of a yoke that is in the long run 'easy,' and 'light.'"*

* Tom Griffith in *Times of Restoration* (Amherst, N.H.: Kingdom Press, January 1987). Used by permission.

Reflections on "A Matter of Timing"

What Tom did:

- stopped dating
- prayed
- accepted a minister's help
- stuck with the church
- hung on
- did not despair
- waited
- bore Christ's yoke steadily

What God did:

- planted a name in Tom's ear
- timed things perfectly

2

She Went with Her Feelings

What he trusts in is fragile;
   what he relies on is a spider's web.
He leans on his web, but it gives way;
   he clings to it, but it does not hold.

Job 8:14–15

Here is a letter from a girl who did what she wished she hadn't.

"The party was wonderful. Four guys to every girl and enough alcohol to fill the ocean. People talked about it for weeks after. It was a great time. Yes, I gained experience, but let me tell you what I lost. I lost everything that was important to me: my health, my witness, my integrity, my money (checks were stolen from me), and my boyfriend. Ah yes—Stan. Let me tell you how I lost Stan. It's simple, really—I cheated on him. He came to the party.

We drank and we made out. I don't know when he left because I passed out. When I woke up at four in the morning there was a very good-looking man in the kitchen. I, loving to initiate, somehow ended up kissing him. By the grace of God I ended up keeping my virginity intact. He too was a virgin and much less experienced than I. I remember his saying that he couldn't take advantage of me as he kissed me and left the room.

"Stan was one of those 'I-believe-there's-a-higher-power-but-I'm-turned-off-by-organized-religion' people. I had grown up in church and knew full well from the beginning that I shouldn't have been with him but the truth is I didn't trust God. Of course I had a personal relationship with God, and I did good deeds, but I failed to realize that deeds without faith are dead. So it was easy for me to cling to someone I could touch and who could touch me! Stan was all I'd dreamed about—handsome, believed a man should be head of the household, and he waited three months to kiss me. I had never before even been with a guy three months. I had this aching insatiable urge, which I now know had come from the Holy Spirit, to confess to him what I had done. When he found out I had kissed that guy in the kitchen it didn't matter about that 'open relationship.' He made it perfectly clear that the only reason we'd had that kind of relationship was that I'd wanted it, and how could I have said I loved him that night and then later destroyed the meaning of the word? He had never said he loved me.

"After we 'broke up' God began opening my eyes to truths about Himself and the lies that I had been living for almost a year. I met a girl who told me the story of Jim Elliot. I didn't pay much attention except for that famous quote about not being a fool for giving up what you cannot keep to gain what you cannot lose. God gave Julie to me to be an example, a strong example of what it meant to trust God. She lent me her copy of *Passion and Purity*. I cannot tell you what a relief it was to hear that crystal clear voice of truth. You see, after Stan and I broke up we began the song and dance of being 'friends.' I thought I had to participate because not to would be weak and besides, I still cared for him, and most importantly, he still cared for me. All of a sudden it became clear to me that what you said, while unpopular with my heart, was consistent with my life. You were tough, unbending, and unyielding to the world view.

"Two days after my twentieth birthday I said yes to God and told Stan to stop touching me. I didn't hear from him for a month. I held tight to your book and often went for a walk with your lecture in my Walkman. More importantly, I held tight to God, whose love was immense.

"Had I not read the passage on initiation and the roles of men and women, I would have been sure to call Stan and demand a confrontation. *Wait on God and shut up* became my motto. I learned so much about Stan from his silence, and more about God by my total committal to Him on that issue.

"The silence from Stan was nearly maddening. Satan filled my head with questions and doubts about whether I had meant anything to him at all. Perhaps there had been a great misunderstanding. Maybe he was waiting for me to call. Satan urged me to find out. After all, I could forget him after I had closure, right? Wrong. Daily God asked me through His word, 'Do you trust Me? Do you love Me?' My answer had to be yes. I would wait on God.

"I was prepared for God's timing to be never, but I've found that God will always test a commitment to Him. That test came four weeks after Stan dropped out of my life. He sent me a sugar-sweet postcard from Key West, saying maybe we could do something when he got back. He carefully signed it 'Your friend,' and addressed me with one of my favorite nicknames, 'Miss Wonderful.' I'd like to say that I passed the test, but I failed. I called him two days later and several more times before I left for overseas. It is not something I am proud of, but God continues to show me that He is all I need and only out of total dependence on Him will I ever be happy.

"Discovering the true power of prayer and seeing a glimpse of God in His perfect timing has filled my cup to overflowing. I now come to Him with buckets.

"It is easy to say that the world doesn't understand, but God is constantly asking me if I am giving them a reason to *want* to understand."

Ours is a longsuffering heavenly Father. Patiently He waits for us to put our trust in Him, never mind what the world would tell us to do, as this story illustrates. Our confusions, mistakes, and disobedience are no surprise to Him.

"Let us then approach the throne of grace with confidence, so that we may receive mercy and find grace to help us in our time of need" (Heb. 4:16).

Reflections on "She Went with Her Feelings"

- Alcohol sabotages the intentions.
- When a woman initiates, confusion ensues.
- An "open relationship," a break-up, then the "song and dance of being friends." Did the decision to trust God change things?
- Can you think of a Scripture that might support the motto, Wait on God and shut up? (Try a verse from a well-known psalm.)

3

God Knows How to Tame Wild Broncos

The LORD will guide you always;
    he will satisfy your needs in a sun-scorched land
    and will strengthen your frame.

Isaiah 58:11

Before Fred Malir became a Christian he was already engaged—to a Christian. She took him to hear the gospel, and his conversion was followed by a call to missionary work. Here was a whole new direction, not one in which his fiancée was prepared to participate. "I don't want to be the wife of a missionary," she said, and that was that.

"A civil war began in my heart that lasted six months," wrote Fred. He lost his joy in the Lord. He felt he could not possibly give up the girl, and the thought of her marrying someone else drove him crazy—but, as he later learned, "God knows how to tame wild broncos."

Patiently He began to soften Fred's heart as he prayed to be made willing to relinquish his beloved. Toward the end of those miserable six months of conflict the Lord "put some godly backbone in my jellyfish nature and I prayed, 'All right, Heavenly Father, I give her up, totally, absolutely, completely!' . . . I discovered that the best way to understand the Holy Scriptures is OBEDIENCE! As soon as I obeyed the Lord, His omnipotent hand, like an expert surgeon, operated on my heart and removed the passion for that girl that was not His will for me. I was truly set free."

Malir went as a missionary, to Montevideo, Uruguay, where he had grown up, but his desire for marriage did not evaporate.

"Twelve long years went by. Then one day when I was traveling in the U.S. God put me next to a born-again Christian girl on a one-hour drive, and the Presence of the dearest Lord Jesus was so vivid in her that I fell in love with Christ in her. For a whole week we were able to see each other often and talk together. We were both conscious that we had fallen in love, but did the Lord want us to be married? Before I was born again, I would kiss a girl first and then would ask myself if I liked her. But now that I was a believer, God made me know that I could not kiss any girl until I was absolutely sure we were going to be married. So I did not kiss Ann.

"I expected some kind of supernatural revelation, like a voice from heaven saying as loud as thunder, MARRY THAT GIRL! But I heard nothing. . . .

"I prayed for a whole week. On a glorious Sunday afternoon, on February 26, 1959, in a way I cannot even explain, I was overwhelmed with the deep assurance from God that He wanted me to marry *Ann*. I did not hear a thunderous voice from heaven, but somehow I had the deep assurance that this was His unmistakable will. I *knew!* But I had a problem: Ann was in Virginia and I was in Uruguay, as far south of the equator as Atlanta is north of the equator. How could I bridge that gap?"

God knows how to bridge gaps. Fred wrote to Ann, telling her of his week of prayer and the clear answer, then signed his name and—imagine this—added a P.S.: *Will you marry me?* For three days he held on to the letter, asking for final confirmation from the Lord. Then he mailed it. Knowing it would be two weeks before he could hear from her, he was astonished to receive a letter a few days later, dated February 26.

He read: "I suppose I will never know until I will meet my Lord in Glory, why He has laid such a burden upon me to pray for you during all this past week. Then today God gave me the assurance that whatever your need was, He had supplied it."

At last came the reply to his proposal: "On the same day the Lord made His will clear to you, He also spoke to me that we were to be married. God made it so plain to me, that I felt like your wife already!"

"And I hadn't even kissed her yet! When we later checked on the days and even the very hour when these things were happening to us, we were amazed to verify that God made known His will to both of us exactly at the same hour. We were moved to write to each other at the same moment. We both held our letters for three days, then mailed them at the same time. Our letters crossed each other in the middle of the air, and we both received each other's letter simultaneously! What a wonderful God we have, and how minutely intricate and detailed is His high-precision guidance for those who seek to know and do His will.

"Now we were engaged—but I had another problem. How could we bridge the 5,300 miles that separated us?"

That question too had its divine answer. Fred Malir was a Uruguayan citizen living in a poor country. He had no money for frills or extras, but three gifts were given him, totaling $162, the equivalent of ten months' salary for a national missionary. What to do with this small fortune? Buy a passage and marry Ann was the answer. *But*—he could find no fare under $400 by either sea or air, until he discovered a one-man, one-plane shuttle service from Buenos Aires to Miami. It was not certified, so nobody wanted to fly it. The owner pared the price down to $162.75. Fred just happened to have seventy-five cents in his pocket.

"I was awed, thrilled, full of joy. My faithful Heavenly Father had provided the needs of His servant to the very penny. By the time I got my papers, packed my luggage and boarded the plane, a dear brother who did not know my needs had given me an envelope with some money—not much, but enough to plunk on the Greyhound counter and say, 'Give me a bus ticket as far as this money will take me toward Lynchburg, Virginia.' It only carried me to Danville, Virginia.

"I was thumbing my way northward on Highway 29 but nobody was picking me up. Three hours I waited. I was very tired and getting discouraged. So I flipped out my Bible, opened it at random and read, 'Whosoever believeth on Him shall not be ashamed' (Rom. 10:11).

"Suddenly, a joyful reaction burst inside me. With happy expectation I prayed, 'Thank you, dearest Heavenly Father, I believe it, I shall not be ashamed, because I trust in You. After all, I did not send myself here. *You* did. So it is *Your* job to take me to Ann's home. Maybe You have me waiting here for a better ride to get me closer. Thank you. I am in Your hands. In the name of the Lord Jesus Christ, Amen.'

"A station wagon stopped. Two painters picked me up. They were on their way to Lynchburg. As I told them about the love of God for man and His provision for washing all our sins through the Lord Jesus Christ's dying on the cross, my painter friends came under conviction. I trust they

31

have since sought out God, repented and believed in Christ as their Lord and Savior.

"They noticed my slight foreign accent and wanted to know why I was in America. I told them that I had come to marry my fiancée, who did not know I was coming and thought that I was 5,300 miles away.

"'You mean you're just going to walk in unannounced?' one of them asked.

"'Yes, I'm going to surprise her!'

"They laughed and suddenly one of them said, 'I'd like to take you to her home.'

"'Oh no,' I protested, 'You fellows are going to work in Lynchburg, and I have some friends there that will be glad to take me to her home. She lives on a farm, quite distant from the main road.'

"He thought it over for a moment, then said, 'Which do you prefer?'

"I was quiet before God for a moment, then slowly answered, 'If you put it that way, then obviously my preference would be to go straight to her house.'"

They took Fred to the farm and waited in the car as he rushed in, his heart beating wildly. Ann, "happening" to be in the next room, opened the door.

All she managed to say was, "*Fred!*"

All Fred could manage was, "*Ann!*"

Fred writes, "In the next moment, we were in each other's arms and that was our first kiss. Suddenly I remembered the painters, still waiting in the car, so we went out to thank them. They were grinning from ear to ear, glad to see that my unusual story was not a figment of my imagination.

"I had five cents in my pocket, no more. But God gave us a big wedding. Our honeymoon began and now, many years later, it still continues, thanks to God."

After nearly forty years Fred met his first fiancée, learned that she had married a non-Christian, and, though having every material benefit, confessed that she was not happy.

He finishes his story with these words: "*Caveat emptor*—Buyers Beware! With these words wary purchasers would warn one another at the market in the times of the old Roman Empire when the merchandise offered might in the long run not turn out to their entire satisfaction. Marriage is a serious business. Why not consult with the Chief Inspector Himself? Only He knows which is the best spouse for us. Otherwise you may think you are getting a *peach* when you are in reality getting a *lemon*. Ask God first. Under no circumstance date a non-Christian—you would be courting disaster."*

* Fred Malir, *Joy* (Box 125, Long Island, VA 24569).

Reflections on "God Knows How to Tame Wild Broncos"

Fred learned:
- It was necessary to relinquish the woman he loved.
- The best way to understand the Holy Scriptures is obedience.
- God knows how to put the right people in the right place at the right time.
- No supernatural revelations are needed.
- Prayer was the key—for him and for her. Both were in touch with God.
- God's timing is perfect.
- God supplies material needs.
- God's guidance included two painters who picked up a hitchhiker.

4

Will and Desire

Because the Sovereign LORD helps me,
I will not be disgraced.
Therefore have I set my face like flint,
and I know I will not be put to shame.

Isaiah 50:7

Fred Malir had prayed that God would help him to be willing to relinquish his beloved. He did not *want* to relinquish her, but he willed to be made willing. Although the conflict lasted for six months, he was indeed helped. God put backbone in his "jellyfish nature" and with a manly thrust he put that girl from him, surrendering her into God's hands.

Obedience brought freedom. But it did not eradicate the man's desire. To hope for marriage is a good thing, a God-given thing, in accord with the human nature God designed. Yet marriage, for some, is not the best thing. Faith receives, day by day, what a loving heavenly Father apportions and leaves to His mercy and judgment the fulfillment or denial of the heart's desires.

> All my longings lie open before you, O Lord;
>   my sighing is not hidden from you.
> My heart pounds, my strength fails me;
>   even the light has gone from my eyes. . . .
> I wait for you, O Lord;
>   you will answer, O Lord my God.
>
> Psalm 38:9–10, 15

He always answers the cry of the man or the woman who *wills* (against all *wanting*) to do His will. It is here that the battle is waged. What do I want? What do I will? which means, what will I do? My will must be baptized with fire—cleansed and purified and *consumed* as I offer it to God, a living sacrifice. Our God is a consuming fire.

"My problem is my heart," writes a twenty-four-year-old, putting her finger precisely on the crucial point where all who would live in God must make their decision. "R. has called me a couple of times in the past few weeks and has let me know that he likes me a lot. I like him too! I really wish God would lead us to marry, but we both feel that this is not what we are being led to do, at least now. As we were praying together he told the Lord, 'Take this relationship as far as You want it to go—or stop it wherever You want.'"

Note the feelings: He likes me. I like him. I really wish. We both feel.

The difficulty is to keep a tight rein on these emotions. They may remain, but it is not they who are to rule the action. They have no authority. A life lived in God is not lived on the plane of the feelings, but of the will. In Scripture the heart *is* the will—it is the man himself, the spring of all action, the ruling power bestowed on him by his Creator, capable of choosing and acting.

The letter continues, "He has years to go before he gets a doctorate and I am committed to a year or more of mission work. I give God my heart and hopes, over and over. But when it comes right down to honest truth I want to get married! I *think* I love this guy. I want to marry him. But he's not asking.

"I see that my deepest desire right now is not for Jesus and His Word, and it's not for mission work. It's for R. This is not right. It's wrong. Why should I want anything more than to do God's will and serve Him, whether married or single? That's where I will be most fulfilled and at peace— *in* His will. I should want to know God most—in His power and in His suffering. My heart should be where His heart is. A marriage that isn't built with God's desires at the center would end up to be ruin for me anyway. My head knows that—but I can't get it through my *heart!*

"I suppose the answer isn't vague—it's probably something like obedience: seeking the Lord in His Word, in prayer, and in serving my family and my church.

"I'm so afraid that if I give up my hopes and dreams they'll never come true! And what if I never marry—will God then take that desire away?

"It's funny—how I forget the things I've read so often, and I sit here trying to figure out what you would say. It's all 'material for sacrifice,' right? But then why does it have to hurt so much?"

Probably by putting into words on paper the turmoil in her heart this woman was beginning to see the answers to her questions.

"Why should I want anything more than to do God's will and serve Him, whether married or single?"

When one makes up one's mind to follow the Lord wholly, it is not uncommon to feel dishonest or hypocritical. The enemy of souls will see to that. If he can persuade us that our wants cancel out our willings he is delighted. Ignore the demonic whisperings and hear the testimony of one man who understood such warfare.

"Though we live in the world, we do not wage war as the world does. The weapons we fight with are not the weapons of the world. On the contrary, they have divine power to demolish strongholds. We demolish arguments and every pretension that sets itself up against the knowledge of God, and we take captive every thought to make it obedient to Christ" (2 Cor. 10:3–5).

Hannah Whitall Smith has a helpful word for that feeling of unreality or hypocrisy.

> Do not be troubled by it. It is only in your emotions, and is not worth a moment's thought. Only see to it that your will is in God's hands, that your inward self is abandoned to His working, that your choice, your decision, is on His side; and there leave it. Your surging emotions, like a tossing vessel at anchor, which by degrees yields to the steady pull of the cable, finding themselves attached to the mighty power of God by the choice of your will, must inevitably come into captivity, and give in their allegiance to Him; and you will sooner or later verify the truth of the saying that, "if any man will do His will he shall know of the doctrine."
>
> *The Christian's Secret of a Happy Life*
> (Grand Rapids: Fleming H. Revell, 1916), 85

"What if I never marry—will God then take that desire away?"

Perhaps He will, quite suddenly and completely, that we may be freed from that burden in order to assume another. Perhaps He will not, in order that we may understand what it means to be "poor in spirit"—aware of our essential poverty and helplessness, having nothing to be proud of, nothing that would encourage us to think well of ourselves. I knew a lady whom God had called to foreign missionary service. She was single. She told the Lord she would gladly serve

37

Him singly, but if it should be His will to give her a husband when she reached retirement age, she would be thankful. The hope remained alive. I attended her wedding to a missionary widower, both of them white-haired by then and full of joy.

"Why does it have to hurt so much?"

My correspondent answered the last question quite specifically: "Yes, I'm a wimpy Christian, and I don't like pain. Sometimes I wish I didn't have to go through this stuff . . . but what about the fellowship of His suffering? I know."

It hurts because it is suffering, real suffering. It would not be suffering if it did not hurt. "In this world," Jesus said, "you will have trouble. But take heart! I have overcome the world" (John 16:33). None of us likes pain. All of us wish at times that we need not "go through all this stuff." Let's settle it once and for all: We cannot know Christ and the power of His resurrection without the fellowship of His suffering.

Often with that thought arises another: Can *my* sufferings have anything to do with His? Because my fickle feelings bring turmoil and sorrow in my life, can I nevertheless hope for some small share in that divine fellowship? The apostle Paul helps us here. There is reason to believe he was at some time married. Was he a widower? Had his wife left him? Or what? He seems to have known more about women than might seem appropriate for a bachelor. He had known many kinds of severe suffering that were directly related to his work for God (and few of our afflictions, I suppose, would fall into *that* category), yet even he says,

> Not that I have already obtained all this, or have already been made perfect, but I press on to take hold of that for which Christ Jesus took hold of me. Brothers, I do not consider myself yet to have taken hold of it. But one thing I do: Forgetting what is behind and straining toward what

is ahead, I press on toward the goal to win the prize for which God has called me heavenward in Christ Jesus.

Philippians 3:12–14

By the grace of God, we can will to do His will. Forget the past. Press toward the goal.

Reflections on "Will and Desire"

- God does not necessarily remove one's desire.
- The psalmist expresses unfulfilled desire as real suffering. Jesus learned obedience not by the things He enjoyed, but by the things that He suffered (see Hebrews 5:8).
- Will and emotion are two separate faculties, both given by God. "What a piece of work is man! How noble in reason! How infinite in faculty!" said Shakespeare.
- Hopes and dreams are material for sacrifice.
- To "take captive every thought" is an act of the will.
- Ponder the metaphor of the pull of the cable.
- Even the apostle Paul had not yet "arrived." He, like the rest of us, had to press on.

5

We Didn't Call It Dating

But now, Lord, what do I look for?
My hope is in you.

Psalm 39:7

"For the last three years I befriended a girl in our church. We're both committed members, each of us leader of a small group that meets in homes. We started off with no intentions of dating or anything of this nature. I was not even attracted to her romantically, but we spent time together doing stuff like running, biking, etc. out of common interest. In January we decided to get to know each other better as friends (brother and sister), nothing more, but over the last year I became more attracted to her as I got to know her. I became *very* attracted to her, even developed a *romantic* attraction.

"Well, over the last three months we began to spend more time together. We didn't call it dating or courting, because we weren't. We just enjoyed each other's company, but in the process we spent a lot of time alone together, or communicating on the phone. We became very intimate and found ourselves sharing more of our deepest feelings, thoughts, etc. with one another. An emotional bond formed between us. I developed a deep love for her and she admitted to me that it was mutual.

"The irony of our relationship is that we weren't even courting for marriage, but I began over time to develop a desire to marry her which I believe, after much prayer, is from God. ('Delight yourself in the Lord and he will give you the desires of your heart' Psalm 37:4.)

"I do desire to be married some day. Through all this she kept telling me she just wanted to be friends, although she had prayed about marrying me if it was the will of God, which she didn't think it was. I know that she has no desire, right now, to marry me or anyone. She's content, and feels she isn't ready—feels God wants her to spend her time building into the lives of the Christian women He has given as friends.

"A week ago over breakfast she told me she didn't think we should be spending time alone and sharing the level of emotional and communicative intimacy that we had been sharing, because she thought that kind of intimacy should be preserved only for marriage. She said we had obligated ourselves to one another without the marital commitment, and our relationship should be redirected.

"This hurt me. It left a big void in my heart. She was my most intimate friend. I have an acute need for close-intimate relationships, but I realize that kind is preserved for marriage where spirit, soul, and body can be shared. I now agree—we need to spend time apart.

"Now we never actually fornicated, but in our hearts we sinned. We acknowledged to each other our struggle to be pure. It was hard, but I decided I would never bring shame on her. ('Lord, who may dwell in your sanctuary? who may live on your holy hill? He whose walk is blameless and who does what is righteous, who speaks the truth from his heart and has no slander on his tongue, who does his neighbor no wrong' Psalm 15:1–3.) We never even kissed, although there were opportunities to do so. Because I love her very much I will not do anything intentionally to hurt her.

"I love her very much. I believe in my heart she is the right one for me. I would like to marry her. We are very compatible. I have decided to seek God and His will for me right now.

"What I would like to know is: Do you think this is unwise to be willing to wait on God to change her heart so that she'll want to marry me?

"Am I presumptuous to think she's the one for me?

"Should I pray that God will make it clear to her and let her confirm it to me?"

Reflections on "We Didn't Call It Dating"

- Identify three steps that led to a "romantic attraction."
- If this pair was not "dating" or "courting," what were they doing? Is there really an irony here, as he suggests?
- How would you answer this man's three questions?

6

Just Friends?

Friend deceives friend,
    and no one speaks the truth.
They have taught their tongues to lie;
    they weary themselves with sinning.
You live in the midst of deception.

Jeremiah 9:5–6

The dangers of a woman's seeking one-to-one friendships with men are many. In the first place, she was not created to be the initiator (more on that later). In the second, all too often she is not being honest with herself about the true motive. Is it *merely* friendship she seeks or something more? In the third place, many a man is quite content to claim he is "just a friend," while often taking advantage of a woman in ways he would not dream of doing with a friend of his own sex.

Here is a woman whose deepest desire is to be a wife and mother. A man dates her for two whole years, expresses his desire someday to have her for a wife. He cannot picture life without her. They go so far as to discuss the manner of engagement—he must ask her father for her hand. Their fellowship, she tells me, was unlike any she had ever known. They decide, after two years, to quit dating in order to "focus on God alone," desiring to "secure undistracted devotion to the Lord," as per 1 Corinthians 7. They stop spending time alone together and try to be "just friends." This, she says, was "incredibly difficult" for her. The man, on the other hand, has no difficulty—his "feelings changed." He no longer wants to marry her.

Then—*presto*—those feelings changed again. He hadn't meant what he said. Now he wants to marry her. But a couple of months later—oops. Another change. Just friends again, but she is, he claims, "very dear" to him, and he is always willing to make small talk when he sees her at church.

Is it possible for a man and a woman, both of whom hope someday to marry someone, to sustain a "just friends" status?

"In the last several years," writes another, "I have felt more discouraged with always having the role of 'good friend' or 'buddy' with men, rather than having my hopes fulfilled in a relationship that could develop into something more serious. Three years ago I met someone and rather quickly discovered that I was falling in love. . . . He had been recently divorced, I wanted to give him space, then it seemed we would just be friends. I began to sense that he was withdrawing. . . .

"One night in prayer I told God I felt like I was at the edge of my faith. I dreamed that night that one of my friends was trying to push me off the top row of the bleachers and I was clinging to the seat, terrified of falling. That dream seemed to illustrate my prayer: I was afraid of turning everything over to God, afraid he wouldn't give me what I wanted, or that if He did I would be hurt. . . .

"Finally he told me he wasn't capable of a serious relationship with anyone, but he wants to spend time with me!! Because of my previous experience with him I have my doubts about that. And today I saw him shopping with a young woman and found out it's someone he has dated. . . . I had a good cry."

I received a beautifully handwritten letter from a woman in Europe, eloquently recounting her love story with a man who gave her every reason to believe he was seriously interested in pursuing her with a view to marriage. Eighteen pages described an exciting relationship, their compatibility, identical goals, lovely times together, increasing evidence that they were moving toward marriage.

One day he said to her, "You're a nice sister."

She was shattered.

Could I help her, she asked, to see what God meant in this?

All of us experience the suffering that comes from someone else's wrongdoing, whether it be intentional or unintentional. It is tempting to refuse forgiveness, or even to blame God for permitting the wrong to happen. E. B. Pusey has given me the following great principle for my life, which I might have given this shattered person.

This, then, is of faith, that everything, the very least, or what seems to us great, every change of the seasons, everything which touches us in mind, body, or estate, whether brought about through this outward senseless nature, or by the will of man, good or bad, is overruled to each of us by the all-holy and all-loving will of God. Whatever befalls us, however it befalls us, we must receive as the will of God. If it befalls us through man's negligence or ill-will or anger, still it is, in even the least circumstance, *to us the will of God* [italics mine]. For if the least thing could happen to us without God's permission, it would be something out of God's control. God's providence or His love would not be what they are. Almighty God Himself would not be the same God; not the God whom we believe, adore, and love.

Mary Wilder Tileston, *Daily Strength for Daily Needs*
(Boston: Little, Brown & Co., 1884), 67

Here's another story.

"Our eyes often met across the office where we worked. One day Jerry came by my desk, asked me to go to coffee break. Of course I was delighted—he's nice-looking, polite, not the sort of guy that comes on strong with all the women. He seemed even a little shy. Reserved is a better word. Over coffee we found out we were both interested in working overseas, teaching English as a foreign language or something.

"I found myself thinking about him a lot, wondering if we could be friends. I know you don't have time to read long stories, so I'll skip a few months. There were a few coffees and we went to the mall one time so I could help him buy a present for his mom. By this time we'd found out we were Christians and both of us were interested in doing work overseas, and I was really shocked when he told me he was going to be a missionary. I ended up helping to support him and his partner for the three months they were over there, so I would write to them, both of them. I didn't want Jerry to think anything. He wrote back once, asking me if I had any plans for overseas, so when his term was up I thought he would call me to talk about it, but he didn't. I waited awhile, thinking it was not my place to call him, but then I called his roommate and Jerry answered. I felt embarrassed because I really didn't want to be interpreted as calling him, but I asked him about the summer, the work, and all.

"Then I didn't hear anything till someone told me he'd been sick. I wondered if there would be anything wrong with calling him just to find out how he was doing. It took me a while to resolve to call him, to talk with myself, tell myself why I was doing this. I guess the final reason I called was because I asked myself this question: 'If it would have been anybody else you had known who was sick, would you call?' The answer was yes, I would call, so I did, and I think he appreciated it.

"I want to be an encourager, a prayer supporter, and he has never expressed any romantic feelings for me at all, in fact all he ever wrote was a note at the bottom of the form letter he sent out to his supporters, warm and friendly, not romantic in any way. I guess what I want to ask your opinion on is what I do with these unruly feelings of mine which I really have a difficult time explaining. But I'll try to spell it out for you as plainly as I can.

1. I deeply respect and am encouraged by Jerry's commitment to God.
2. I want to be excited for him in his personal life, even if he dates and marries another girl, I want to rejoice because I know those two will be a dynamite team for Jesus! And deep in my heart what I want is to see Jerry continue to be used by God to reach people with the saving message of the Gospel. I don't want my feelings or desires to ever question or demand of God what I think I would like to see. God knows what is best.
3. I wanted to write Jerry back right away, but I think that is too forward, so I wrote, didn't date my letter, and I resolved to wait for two or three weeks before I mailed it.
4. When he wrote to say he's joining the mission full-time I found myself saying, 'Lord, he's the one. I'll take him. Thank You,' because that kind of ministry has been where my heart is.

5. In my limited scope of vision I see absolutely no way to get to know him. I will be in California for at least two more years.

"So I wonder—am I frustrated, am I hoping? Hmmm. I guess what I would like is to know him better but to maintain a brother-sister relationship. I want to come across as a sister and that's what I want to be.

"Should I keep on writing?

"How can I encourage and not manipulate?

"What needs can I meet or that the Lord would have me meet here in California?"

The hope for a husband is there, clear as the sky: "I'll take him." The frustration follows inevitably: "I want to maintain a brother-sister relationship." The duplicity is obvious.

Reflections on "Just Friends?"

- When two adults "date" for two years it can be habit-forming. Note the result in the first story of this chapter.
- A certain pattern often seems to emerge when a man and woman claim they are "just friends." Describe it.
- Discuss the statements: "I didn't want Jerry to think anything" and "I really didn't want to be interpreted as calling him."
- If you were Jerry, would you think anything? How would you interpret the call?

7

The Trouble
with Relationships

Do not let your tongue lead you into sin, and then say
before the angel of God that it was a mistake.

Ecclesiastes 5:6

The beginning of trouble is the use of the word *relationship*. People say, "I'm in a relationship." A mother does not
say she is "in a relationship" with her child. It is a God-
ordained relationship and therefore understood, as are all
other relationships such as teacher/pupil, employer/
employee, king/subject, husband/wife, brother/sister.
While Christians may properly think of themselves as members of the family of God, and therefore related to the rest
as fathers and mothers in the faith, or brothers and sisters,
no one speaks of being "in a relationship" when one belongs
to one of those divinely designated categories. While I am
a member of my pastor's flock, I do not say I am "in" a

relationship with my pastor. If I did, the whole church would be buzzing.

A woman in her thirties told me she had fallen in love with a man who was "not willing to commit to a relationship." This raised puzzling questions in my mind. For example:

Did he volunteer this information, or did she ask him for a commitment?
Did she explain what she meant by *commit?*
What would be her expectations?
Did either of them define *relationship?*

She didn't say.

"So we kept it on a friendship level. I really felt he needed a friend and I felt like I was supposed to be that friend." The man was hurt by events in his life, turned bitter, drifted away from God, "but I still felt an obligation to be his friend. I just wanted to be there for him. Well, we got involved physically—too far. I had always been very pure before the Lord, so falling into immorality brought a lot of shame. I was in a very, very vulnerable place."

When a Christian woman offers her sympathy to a man who has turned away from God she is indeed in a very vulnerable place. Would she say she was in a relationship? Brother/sister? Just friends? Something else?

"But he wouldn't take no for an answer. I would fight, but I would always give in. Then I would feel guilty and would come back to patch things up. I felt responsible for the success of our relationship—what he needed was a friend. He knows I love him, but at the same time I have told him that more than that, I just want to be his friend.

"How does one handle the desire for marriage when year after year relationships don't work out?"

50

The desire for marriage is a good and natural one. Once in a while we hear a young person say that he's giving up dating for *x*-number of weeks or months. A seminary student told us he was quitting the dating scene for the whole of the coming school year. We congratulated him. He's a very attractive man who has had some very attractive girlfriends. The distraction from studies was considerable. The decision was commendable. In less than a month he mentioned having taken a girl to dinner.

"A *date?*" we asked.

"Oh no. Just friends."

Very soon he was head-over-heels. So much for his strength of will to follow through on a decision.

A young woman told us she had decided to take a year off dating and romance. We agreed that this was a good idea. But she had a problem. She hoped for "friendships." Further conversation revealed that it was, not surprisingly, friendships with the opposite sex she was talking about. It didn't work. Few of them do, for any length of time. One of the two who are "just friends" soon becomes interested in something more.

"When guys found out I wasn't into dating they weren't interested in friendships."

Precision in definitions would help.

It happened that a man this girl admired asked her for a date. That was the end of her "year off."

"I faltered in my commitment to God. I rationalized: My primary attraction to him was his faith."

One can hardly help feeling a bit skeptical. *Primary* attraction—faith? Perhaps. But the heart is a lonely hunter, "the most deceitful of all things, desperately sick; who can fathom it?" (Jer. 17:9 NEB).

If men and women would face honestly their real motives, many a pitfall would be avoided.

A married woman describes a great deal of emotional stress at home, including deep trouble with her husband, so: "I've been going to the gym to work out. The exercise, I thought, would help. I'm scared and lonely. I met a man there and we got to be really good friends. He's in a rocky relationship and needs someone to talk to, so we've had some real in-depth conversations which I think have really been good for us. But we did go too far. We had sex. Now I feel guilty. What should I do?"

She feels guilty because she is guilty.

The answer, of course, is contained in one word: Repent. That means an about-face. A dead stop, a 180-degree turn. *Run* in the opposite direction, which, to be very realistic in such a case, would mean never to go back to the gym. Wouldn't a long brisk walk with God outdoors each day have been a safer remedy for the emotional stress? Perhaps she lives in a dangerous big city. Try aerobics by running up and down stairs, or get a trampoline! Either is cheaper than membership in a health club.

I once wrote, "If your passions are aroused, say so—to yourself and to God, *not* to the object of your passion."

A girl who had read that statement had questions.

"1. When do you and how do you let it be known? Only after he states his intentions, or only when he asks? Many men won't say anything for the longest time!"

A forthright proposal, *Will you marry me?* provides the best opportunity to let your feelings be known. It is up to the initiator to make that. A true man will make up his mind sooner rather than later.

"2. Isn't it being deceptive if you don't tell him how you feel?"

He has no right to know until he has told you how he feels, which ought to accompany his proposal. My father taught my four brothers that they should never tell a woman "I love you" until they were ready to follow that declaration with an immediate, "Will you marry me?"

"3. What if you don't suspect any 'romantic spark' on his part, but there is on yours? How do you keep your emotions from progressing?"

Keep him at arm's length was my mother's advice. I would add that emotions can best be kept in check by bringing them under the authority of Christ. See 2 Corinthians 10:5.

"4. At what point (if ever) do you say, 'It's really hard for me to spend time with you without knowing your feelings'? And if he says, 'Just friends,' do you say, 'It's too hard for me to spend time with you as friends because my heart yearns for more and it only gives me hope'? Can I tell friends my feelings?"

Questions like that take the initiative. If it's true that it's hard, stop seeing the man. If he loves you, he will pursue you more specifically.

Best not to tell anyone your feelings for him. Chances are great that word will get back to him, which is perhaps just what you want.

"5. What if you've been going out with a guy and you sense there's interest on his part, but not on yours? You haven't done anything besides be nice and have fun, but are afraid he hopes for more and don't want to lead him on. How do you tactfully let him know that there's no romance in your heart if he hasn't verbally stated his intent?"

Don't accept another date with him. He'll catch on after a couple of refusals.

"6. And if he does say he wants more and you tell him you don't—and he says, 'that's fine,' but you sense he's still hoping, how do you avoid keeping that hope alive? Insist he not pay your way? Insist on not going out? Give up on the friendship altogether?"

See answer to question five.

"7. About calling men: Is it okay if (and only if) there is absolutely no intent or hope for more? Like calling a friend to play racquetball or to grab a bite to eat or to talk."

Not a good idea.

"8. And what about the ones who have made it clear in the past that they were interested, but you didn't reciprocate—is it toying with them to hope you can keep the friendship?"

Yes.

"9. What about calling someone I'd like for something to happen between us to invite to group functions. I know, of course, that somebody else can call him, or he can initiate if he really wants to become involved with the group like he says he does."

Let him initiate.

"10. What about calling him for a 'group date' where the women pay?"

Group dates are fine as long as it's the men who had the idea, the men who call, and the men who pick up the tab. This is what a date is about. If it's just a gang of friends going out after church, for example, where there has been no advance planning, it's not a date. Each pays for his own food.

"11. Do I always have to let him pay? I think it may put unnecessary pressure on him. Am I stepping out of bounds to say, 'I'll pay my way'?"

If you sense pressure, suggest that you go to McDonald's. Better to go where he can afford the tab.

"12. If he is pursuing me just to have someone to do things with whenever he wants to, but I'd love to have more, is it right for me to let him pay—since *he* called? Otherwise I won't call him because he'll be afraid I'm chasing. Should I just forget my hopes and treat him as just a friend (i.e., not be afraid to call or pay my way)? I think I can honestly say that I'd rather have a friendship and no romance, than no friendship at all."

What else can I say?

"13. Does it have to be the man pursuing a *friendship* too? It's my nature to reach out to include others, but do I stifle it if they're male?"

Who would have dreamed that men and women could create such complexities for themselves? When the "ancient paths" are overgrown things do get terribly complicated. There's nothing new about that. Long ago the prophet Jeremiah spoke:

> "Turn from your evil ways, each one of you, and reform your ways and your actions." But they will reply, "It's no use. We will continue with our own plans; each of us will follow the stubbornness of his evil heart." Therefore this is what the LORD says:
>
> > "My people have forgotten me;
> >   they burn incense to worthless idols,
> > which made them stumble in their ways
> >   and in the ancient paths."
>
> Jeremiah 18:11–13, 15

Here is the simple way.

"I once read an article of yours in a magazine about not pursuing men—'Don't leave little messages in his box, don't do anything.' Wow! DID THAT STOP ME!! I was caught in that little and powerful snare of doing nice things in hope. I went to the Lord and asked for forgiveness and help in changing that. Seven years later God brought along a man who was attracted to me because I was 'a virtuous woman who was looking for God's will in my life.' The man is the hunter and provider, and it was so wonderful to be able just to rest and leave it on the altar, not having to do anything but seek God and respond.

"I have shared your understanding with other single women who were seeking peace in this area of surrender."

My answers have perhaps been infuriatingly blunt. Is a true friendship impossible between one man and one woman? Not for the truly holy. Hear the words of a holy man, St. Francis de Sales, who in his wisdom-packed book, *Introduction to the Devout Life,* writes:

> Holy friendship has no looks but what are simple and modest, no caresses but those that are pure and sincere, no sighs but for heaven, no familiarities but those of the soul, no complaints but that God is not loved, the infallible signs of purity.
>
> Worldly friendship confuses the judgment. . . . Holy friendship has a clear light and does not seek to hide itself, appearing willingly before good men.
>
> When we see a man dress himself out and draw near to flatter and wheedle, and whisper in the ears of a woman with no pretension to lawful marriage, without doubt it is in order to incite her to impurity; and a virtuous woman will close her ears to the voice of the charmer who seeks to enchant her: but if she hearken to him, what an ominous sign it is of the future loss of her heart!
>
> Young people who indulge in looks and caresses, or speak words in which they would be unwilling to be surprised (i.e., overheard) by their fathers, mothers, husbands or wives, bear witness that their conduct is not that of honor and conscience. The Virgin Mary was troubled on seeing an angel in human form because she was alone, and he praised her greatly although his praise was heavenly. O Savior of the world! Purity fears an angel in the form of a man; why then does not purity fear a man even in angelic form, when he pours forth praises sensual and human?

(New York: Joseph F. Wagner, Inc., 1923), 176–78

Reflections on "The Trouble with Relationships"

- Clarify your own thinking on the word *relationship*.
- In the presence of God think what kind of relationship you most desire.
- Is it dangerous for a woman to offer sympathy to a man? What about vice versa? Why?
- When a man or a woman believes he/she is ready for marriage, does it matter (very much? at all?) who initiates?
- Write your own answers to the girl's thirteen questions in this chapter.

8

What Is a Date?

There are three things that are too amazing for me,
  four that I do not understand:
the way of an eagle in the sky,
  the way of a snake on a rock,
the way of a ship on the high seas,
  and the way of a man with a maiden.

Proverbs 30:18–19

In thousands of fitness centers across the country men in shorts and T-shirts, women encased in expensive, gleaming skin-tight sheathes move to a thundering beat. The scene is bodies in motion—all sorts and conditions of bodies, but those generally up front, under the brightest lights, are the males with the rippling muscles and the svelte, sylphlike females with the stunningly provocative thong leotards. Farther back are the ponderous soft ones who jiggle.

One of the men, drenched in sweat and panting, punches furiously into the air, while a panting woman near him bounces with serious concentration through an aerobics routine. They do not look at each other but after class they will go out for sushi. They are on a date. Owners of these clubs report an increasing number of dating couples in their classes. "Sometimes they kiss good-bye as they walk into the locker room," said one.

Is it possible that the gym will replace the movie theater and the restaurant as the place to date? Hard to imagine. Who, we wonder, finds it attractive to watch women sweat?

"Whether a gym date is a turn-on or a turn-off seems to depend partly on how one feels about perspiration," one newspaper columnist said. "An arts project director in New York likes it. She found the experience of working out with a date 'sexy—the taut muscles, the sweating together, the smells.'" "A real old-fashioned girl!" commented the man who sent me the clipping.

I had my first date (and, as it turned out, one of the few I ever had) when I was in the eighth grade in 1939. This meant that a boy asked me to go to a party with him. It happened to be a Halloween party at the church, and he came to my house, rang the doorbell, and was ushered into the living room to meet my parents. They told him what time they expected him to bring their daughter home. Off we went, on foot, of course, to the church. We had a good time till somebody suggested kissing games. At that we decided it was time to leave. Ned took me straight home.

It was all very simple, and I can't recall any uncetainty about the procedure. It was as follows:

1. Boy asks girl, not the reverse.
2. He has a definite plan for the evening.
3. She has her parents' permission to say yes.
4. He dresses like a gentleman and behaves like a gentleman.

5. There is no physical contact at all.
6. He complies with the curfew rule.

Between the ages of fourteen and seventeen I attended a boarding school in the South where there was considerable emphasis on learning to be ladies and gentlemen. Most extra-curricular activities were for the student body as a whole, but certain specified occasions were for "dating." In order to discourage "going steady," or any show of favoritism, boys were not allowed to date the same girl twice in a row, and girls could not refuse a date when asked. This enabled all the boys and girls to learn how to treat each other socially, under close faculty supervision, and have a harmless good time in the learning. We were met by our dates at the foot of the stairs, under the eyes of faculty members seated nearby. We said goodnight at the same spot.

Laughable? Yes, preposterous in today's world. Crazy. Unnatural. Antiquated. And *impossible.* You can't go back.

Are we sure about that?

Strange that most of us allow society to dictate most of the rules. Fashion dictates. Peer groups dictate. Economics, professions, political parties, country clubs, the mass media all dictate what we should think, wear, buy, eat, drink, watch, drive, smoke, print, read, say, sleep in, sit on, stand for, march for, and strike for, not to mention *believe.* If we happen to be among those who believe things that society in general scorns, are we right to fall in line with that society's notions about courtship and marriage?

As for the word *dating,* although it is still in use, it seems indefinable as to procedure. One woman described dating as "serial courtships that include kissing everyone you go out with," a prospect that left her so downhearted she decided she would no longer have any part in it. A broken engagement ten years earlier had left her extremely depressed. She finally discovered the reason for the persistent depression: "We did everything but go 'all the way.' We would 'neck' for hours at a time. Now I realize how sinful and mutually destructive this was. A big load has been taken off my shoulders!"

There was a time, as I have shown, when the procedure for a date was perfectly clear. The purpose was also understood. It was a social engagement between two people of opposite sex. It was the beginning of an approach to marriage.

Marriage itself has fallen on very hard times. Small wonder that dating and courtship have also. We used to believe that boys and girls, men and women, must learn somehow to behave themselves properly with each other. The rubrics are now in tatters, as the following letter demonstrates.

"I have read *Passion and Purity* and your books on masculinity and femininity [*The Mark of a Man* and *Let Me Be a Woman*] and I've listened to your interviews with Dobson—all umpteen times. My heart absolutely leaps with excitement in agreement with the things you say. It goes, 'YEAH! That's the way it *should* be!!' Unfortunately, I am finding out that that's not the way it *is*. Instead of men being strong in the Lord, leaders, hunters, taking the initiative (their God-ordained role), they are becoming weak, insecure, afraid of rejection, and not wanting to take a risk—even to make a simple phone call or invitation. They say 'I'll call you' and then they don't.

"I want to believe in God's order, but where is it anymore? While I sit waiting for a strong, secure man to enter my life without fear (someone willing to swim against the tide, *find out* if I'd be interested in him, even though I'm not letting on that I am), simply because he knows the meaning of loving and cherishing a woman and wants to give of himself to another—you know who's getting the guys??? (I hate the word 'get'—it sounds as though you have to earn a relationship, like God isn't even involved!)

The girls who are obvious are getting the guys. They may even be doing the calling and asking. It seems like the girls who *used* to win the guys were the ones who didn't act interested, yet the guys just kept trying.

"And as for your mother's rule, 'Don't chase boys, and keep them at arm's length,' I've been attempting to keep those rules and achieved little lasting results. After a usual one and only date, friends tell me, 'Maybe you didn't act interested enough; maybe your looks, spirituality, or purity intimidated him; maybe he's shy and is waiting for you to make the next move; maybe you were too, too, too; maybe you were not enough . . . and on and on.

"I get so confused with what I'm supposed to do or not do, I am ready to forget this whole dating and getting acquainted business. Where's the persistence, the determination to win a girl's heart and trust, cost what it will? Where's the peace, surety, confidence, fun, anticipation? Do we have to become aggressive because the men aren't? I try to be a lady, in the hope that the guy will be equally as much a man.

"I feel like I just don't know how to play the game anymore. I don't know the rules. Time's awastin'! Maybe I'm playing by an obsolete set of rules while the modern age is playing by new ones. I used to know, but that was long ago, before I became a Christian. Now, when I'm supposed to let God have control, it's just gotten harder and more unsettling. I actually get sick to my stomach trying to figure it all out. I know you're very busy, but any time out you could take would be appreciated. Maybe it won't be wasted time because you'd be helping a lost soul and perhaps you could write another book with my double-minded questions and your solid input."

Very many letters I receive prove how drastically times have changed. "The American way of dating," writes a young man, "STINKS! The whole basis of it is wrong—looking for someone who will meet your needs and satisfy you, instead of looking to truly love and give and build up."

Dating is not only highly confusing but obviously very dangerous. It is generally taken for granted that dating means sex. One graduate of an Ivy League college told me that only one man had asked her out a second time. The others, learning that she would not go to bed, never called again. The one who did call thought perhaps she was just being coy. He thought that on the second date she might be persuaded. Against all odds this woman preserved her virginity, and on her wedding day was able to wear its timeless symbol, the white veil, *honestly.*

It seems that "recreational" dating has no intention of seriousness. One advertisement in the Personals column of a newspaper captures the spirit:

> Are you under forty? Or look it? WF, intelligent, conversant (erudite a plus), very pretty a necessity, beautiful even better, and if gorgeous that would be optimum, coupled with a great figure and an alive personality and would like to make periodic first class weekend and vacation trips to sun resorts both in and away from the U.S. for the fun of it, accompanying me, a fiftyish, good-looking, physically fit semi-retired business man who enjoys the outdoors and does all sports, likes the better things in life and knows how to treat a lady. For the time being I'm not interested in a conditional relationship or long term commitment. I simply want to pursue my hedonistic and romantic inclinations with a sensuous companion, free from time to time to share Hassle-Free quality fun trysts for as long as they last. If you fit the bill, then go for it. Note and photo would be nice.

Hassle-free quality fun trysts! Yet I imagine a number of women took the hook.

Another wrote to an advice columnist, "I get so tired of women always wanting to get serious. I enjoy women, and like to date, but all I want is a little diversion and a few laughs." The columnist's advice: "Take a hyena to lunch."

Reflections on "What Is a Date?"

- Define a date. It might be interesting to note how members of the opposite sex define it.
- True or false:

  1. Dating is the best approach to marriage.
  2. Dating is the only available approach to marriage.
  3. Dating is not meant to be an approach to marriage.

- Can you suggest alternatives to dating?
- See Ephesians 4:17–20. Ask yourself what difference there is, if any, between your thinking on this subject of dating and a non-believer's.

9

A Praying Father's Word

My [daughter], if you accept my words
and store up my commands within you,
turning your ear to wisdom
and applying your heart to understanding,
and if you call out for insight
and cry aloud for understanding,
and if you look for it as for silver
and search for it as for hidden treasure,
then you will understand the fear of the LORD
and find the knowledge of God.

Proverbs 2:1–5

"No dating until you're sixteen," Faith's parents had said.

When Faith reached that age, she began immediately to date Jack, a boy she had always admired, who was seventeen. He was popular in school and a leader in the church youth group. On a trip to Europe with her father, Faith decided she wanted to join a mission after graduation. Jack seemed to share her enthusiasm but he had a different mission in mind. Things began to go downhill as they became emotionally attached. Realizing the danger, Faith chose a college that would take her farther away from Jack, who then offered to buy her an engagement ring. Faith refused, explaining that she wanted to date other boys in college. Jack promised to wait for her.

"I knew I didn't want to marry him but I liked having him around. I was *using* him. I didn't tell him I never intended to marry him. All the while, my conscience was bothering me and I sensed this situation as not pleasing to God."

A missionary who was a guest in Faith's home observed Jack's attentions. The missionary asked her when she and Jack were to be married.

"Oh," she said, "I don't plan on *ever* marrying him!"

She never forgot that missionary's reply. Boldly he told her it was wrong to lead a man on in this way. Dating, he said, was for the purpose of finding a life's mate, *"period!"* She was irritated but could not dismiss his words. Although she dated some nice men in college, no serious relationship developed.

One morning during the summer after her graduation Faith, on her way to the bathroom, noticed her father kneeling by his bed praying. There was nothing unusual about that, but as she washed her face, she thanked the Lord for such a father, and for his godly example.

At that moment he came to the bathroom door, which was open, and told her he had something important to tell her. She was "all ears."

"Now I'm going to tell you something, Faithie," he said, "and after I tell you this, I don't want you to ask me any questions—okay?"

She nodded.

"Faithie, a year from now you're going to be a happily married woman."

And with that he left.

The girl stood there in awe. Her father was not a charismatic man. He did not see visions or speak in tongues and was skeptical of those who claimed to have a "word of knowledge." He had not said that *God* had given him this information, but she felt that He must have. She was excited.

A new Bible school was to be opened that fall, and Faith had been asked to help with the task of getting it ready and then of supervising the dozen or so women who would attend. She was delighted to discover that Ed, a fine young man whom she had met in her last semester in college, was in charge of the men. Hope began to rise, but to Faith's dismay, he kept his distance. At twenty-two, with most of her friends marrying, she felt like an "old maid." After some days of wrestling with God on the matter, she came to the point of cheerfully telling Him that if He wanted her to remain single for the rest of her life, she would accept that. "And I meant it!" she said.

Two weeks later the first student arrived. His name was Dave, picked up at the airport by none other than Ed. The two men found her scrubbing toilets—a great scene for an introduction.

"I was embarrassed," she wrote. "I looked a wreck with my cleaning clothes on."

Although dating was not prohibited at that school, it simply was not done. Students studied together, worked in the kitchen, ate together, cleaned up afterwards, played ping-pong, and worshiped together.

"From the moment I met Dave I was impressed with him. He had only been a Christian for a year but was unlike any other Christian I'd ever met. He certainly didn't take his new life in Christ for granted. He was very kind and always did his kitchen duty and other chores cheerfully. He seemed rather quiet and very serious. He spent every spare minute in his room studying. He was also very handsome. All the girls, including me, were nuts about him.

Once I heard him talking with some of the other fellows about celibacy and its benefits. It was admirable, but my heart sank.

"My dad came to the school as a guest lecturer in November, and I told him about Dave and how neat he was. Every evening during that week Dad would take a handful of students out with him for a bite to eat. All the students got a turn, but Dad asked Dave to go with him every single night! And me too! I never knew it until years later, but on the day Dad left, he came into the classroom and said good-bye to everyone and asked Dave to come out into the hall.

"You know, Dave,' he said, 'you're just the kind of young man I've always hoped my Faithie would marry.' Then he gave him a wink and was off. My dad is such a character! I'd have been mortified if I'd known that at the time."

Perhaps sensing Faith's interest in Dave, her friend Ed surfaced again and even went so far as to propose to her. She put him off. A month later he gave her an ultimatum: Make up your mind now or never. This was tough. Dave was nice to her—and to all the women but showed no special interest in any.

"Still," thought Faith, "I'd rather take my chances." She told Ed, "Sorry, but no," hoping desperately that she had made the right decision.

"That very same day after class, Dave asked me if I'd meet him in the sanctuary that evening at seven o'clock. I said 'sure.' I had no idea what he wanted to talk about.

"At seven P.M. I walked over to the church and Dave met me at the door and said, 'Could you come back at seven-thirty?' Sure. At seven-twenty-five the phone rings. One of the other girls gets it. 'Faith, that was Dave. He said to come over at eight.' What in the world was this all about?

"At eight I walked over to the church, Dave meets me at the door, seems very nervous. We walk into the sanctuary and sit down up on the platform. Then he gets up and says, 'I'll be right back.' Five long minutes later he's back.

"'What did you want to talk about, Dave?'

"'I've been trying to get ahold of your parents on the phone. I was wondering (pause) if you'd give me the privilege of being your husband?'

"Without any hesitation I said yes. We embraced and kissed for the first time. It was unbelievable. When we announced our engagement the next day all the students were in shock. They couldn't believe it. Neither could I. I had never been so happy.

"Dave wanted to get married in a month (March) but when we talked to my parents, my mother insisted we wait until June, so that she could plan a nice wedding. A big wedding wasn't what Dave had in mind, but he kept my mom happy.

"June 3, 1978, a little more than eight months after we met, we were married. Dad's little prophecy was correct.

"I tell you, my husband Dave isn't perfect, but he's about as close as you can get. I thank God for him every day."

Reflections on "A Praying Father's Word"

- Here is a man of prayer. . . .
- And a girl who respected her father.
- Here is an observant man. With his daughter's best interest at heart and his awareness of a father's responsibility to help her toward marriage, he took note of Faith's interest and he arranged an opportunity to watch Dave.
- God used a third party to bring two people together.

10

A Harmony
of Differences

The husband is the head of the wife as Christ is the head
of the church, his body, of which he is the Savior. Now as
the church submits to Christ, so also wives should submit
to their husbands in everything.

Ephesians 5:23–24

One of the most memorable letters I've had came from a
physician engaged to a physician. Both are in the Royal
Air Force.

"God has been unbelievably gracious to us both," she
wrote. "Having made many mistakes in the past, it's such
a wonderful example of the peace and freedom we experience when obeying our Heavenly Father.

"I've been posted in Germany for the last six months
and my fiancé is in England. Your first husband's letters
[in *Passion and Purity*] now ring very true: 'Let not our

longing slay the appetite of our living.' I've certainly tried to follow that advice. . . .

"Whilst out bush-walking up in the North West of Australia we stopped at an old man's hut. He lived alone, hundreds of miles from any civilization. He was a Christian and prayed with us after insisting that we have a cup of tea with him. In his dark, dusty hut he had piles of books. Intrigued, I passed my eyes over his selection. . . . I commented on them, looking at the then unknown titles: *Let Me Be a Woman* and *The Mark of a Man*. He explained that he lent them to young aboriginal guys and gals to show them how Jesus wants them to live. How marvelous! . . .

"On returning to England I finally tracked down copies of both the above books. Without boring you with the details may I simply say they probably helped me more than I can comprehend. They restored in me a delight in my femininity, something a rather hardened and confused young lady had somehow lost. Furthermore an acceptance of God's design that man and woman are different. Let us enjoy the differences, not fight them. If I hadn't come to feel this I'm sure I wouldn't be engaged today.

"Even up until a year ago I was pretty convinced I was going to be single. I had apparently received the 'gift of singleness,' as I was not concerned about seeking a husband! I'm delighted to say that due to this state of mind my now fiancé did the initiating/chasing, and I simply enjoyed it!

"In the medical profession I am bombarded each day with the world's fallen demands and expectations. Professional colleagues can't even conceive of considering God's part in our lives and how we lead them. . . . Please keep the books coming!"

The books this correspondent had come across in the hut celebrate the glorious inequalities of femininity and masculinity. The first was written as a wedding present to my daughter Valerie, since she belonged to a generation that was becoming increasingly confused about the differences between men and women, thanks to the rise of radical feminism that was dedicated at least to smudging if not actually to abolishing that enormously significant distinction. The most surprising response to that book came from men who told me they had learned much about what it means to be a *man* through reading it. Well, I mused—it does take a tough man to walk around with a book entitled *Let Me Be a Woman* under his arm! Maybe I should write one specifically for men. *The Mark of a Man,* addressed to my nephew Peter deVries, presents what I trust is a biblical view of masculinity.

In a world where men get together out in the woods to bang drums, shriek and bellow and cry on each other's shoulders, and where women loudly declare, often in weird ways, that they don't need men, ambivalence about "roles" is not surprising. If a man and woman have lunch together, each wonders, "Will he/she freak out if I offer to pay? or if I *don't* offer to pay?" I tried to show the importance of the divine *order,* the wonderfully differing designs and functions of male and female, and the necessity of recognizing that the whole universe is constructed on the principle of hierarchy (God, cherubim, seraphim, archangels, angels, men—"a little lower than the angels"—and animals), an idea that is anathema to most of our society.

Yet "subordination is not inferiority," wrote P. T. Forsyth.

It is divine. The principle has its roots in the very cohesion of the Eternal Trinity. . . . To recognize no lord or master is satanic. . . . I insist on the Christian principle, drawn from the very nature of God and essential to the masculinity and femininity which He has made. Without the spirit of subordination there is no true piety, no manly nobility, and no womanly charm.

"Gender is a reality, and a more fundamental reality than sex," writes C. S. Lewis in *Perelandra.*

> Sex is, in fact, merely the adaptation to organic life of a fundamental polarity which divides all created beings. Female sex is simply one of the things that have feminine gender; there are many others, and Masculine and Feminine meet us on planes of reality where male and female would be simply meaningless.

(New York: Macmillan, 1965), 200

Philip Zaleski, who teaches religion at Smith College and English at Wesleyan University, administers what he calls "a peculiar little test" to his nature writing students. He offers a list of fifteen items:

mouse
boy
sun
angel
ant
crab
Norwegian pine
corn
amoeba
hamburger
potato
Moby Dick
Taj Mahal
Rolls Royce
the idea of the good

and he asks the students to rank them, using whatever scale they deem most important. The great majority always put the sun at the top. When the professor presses them to explain why, they allow that they order according to what we must call *being*.

While the *idea* of hierarchy has been tragically lost in our modern world, the *sense* remains. Everybody knows that cabbages and kings are neither equal nor interchangeable. But are men and women, by virtue of being human, interchangeable?

A girl who had told me I was "tough, unbending, and unyielding" also told me, "I came into a situation where rumors were flying around about a good Christian friend and myself. There were people who thought that we should date and that he 'looked different' when he said my name. My temptation to initiate brought me close to ruining the only friendship I had ever had with a male that was truly from God. I cringe to think of what could have happened had I not had you to *beg* me to wait on God. . . . Daily God asked me, Do you trust Me? Do you love Me? My answer had to be yes. I would wait on God."

The loss of the idea of hierarchy (from the Greek *hieros*, "sacred," and *arche*, "rule" or "origin") has wrought havoc. Men suffer. If they soft-pedal their masculinity, they're wimps. If they don't, they're M.C.P.s (male chauvinist you-know-whats). If they come on strong, they're macho. If they try to be gentlemen, they run the risk of insulting a woman who demands equality. ("Did you open that door for me because I'm a *lady?*" asked one belligerent college student of a male professor. "No," was the reply, "I opened it because I'm a gentleman.") If they wait for the women to be the aggressors, they lose self-respect or suffer a bad case of identity crisis—who am I? man or mouse?

Women suffer. They want equality in job opportunities and pay. They want power and freedom, but most of them also want to be sought and wooed and taken care of and cherished and, in a word, married. They've been looking for fulfillment Out There, and at the same time longing for fulfillment In Here.

Zaleski sees in the *loss of hierarchy* consequences of the gravest kind: the collapse of the family, acceptance of abortion, unrestricted sexual indulgence, violence, murder, and torture. (For his views, see his article, "A Peculiar Little Test," *First Things,* January 1994.)

Small wonder, then, that the dating scene is a mess. There is a right way and a wrong way to do just about everything. God is not the author of confusion. He assigned to men the higher place and thereby liberated us women. The sexual differences are not limited to mere anatomy.

Reflections on "A Harmony of Differences"

- The passage from Ephesians 5 that introduces this chapter contains the kernel of the argument for masculine initiation and feminine response. Can you state the connection?
- Is the divine assignment of the husband's headship and the wife's submission based on competence?
- Which one, in your opinion, is assigned the harder task? Explain your answer.
- Study Forsyth's statement, "Without the spirit of subordination there is no true piety, no manly nobility, and no womanly charm."
- Does the idea of rank or hierarchy make you:
    a. thankful, b. irritated, c. relieved, or what?

11

When Women Initiate

Youths oppress my people,
women rule over them.
O my people, your guides lead you astray;
they turn you from the path. . . .
The women of Zion are haughty,
walking along with outstretched necks,
flirting with their eyes.

Isaiah 3:12, 16

A movie being filmed as this chapter is written deals, according to the newspaper, with sexual harassment of men by
women. A certain pair had long been lovers. Now she is
his boss. Despite his having a wife, the sexually aggressive
boss plots to get him horizontal again. The fact that this
scenario arouses more discussion than the reverse only
indicates that society in general finds it somehow a bit
more bizarre and amusing. Even some of those who claim
equality of the sexes, and would sneer at the idea that

casual sex is wrong, may still feel that men, not women, ought to be the wooers.

This is not a book about marriage. It is about approaching marriage. The way of a man with a maiden ought to take into account the differences between men and maidens.

God created Adam first. Then, seeing the one thing that He labeled "not good" in His creation—that the man should be alone—He created a creature marvelously like and marvelously *unlike* that man.

She was made *for* the man.

She was made literally *from* the man ("bone of his bone").

She was brought *to* the man.

She was named *by* the man.

Was she not "equal" to the man? Yes—in three specific ways:

Both were made by God.

Both were made in the image of God.

Both were placed under moral responsibility.

But the two are also notably "unequal" and, as I see it, *gloriously* unequal. Not competitive but complementary. Have you watched a man and a woman waltzing? We did, in Vienna—a professional pair. What beauty! What grace! What harmony and complementariness! What a lovely paradigm of graceful rule and glad submission! If the woman had suddenly made up her mind to lead, the whole thing would have been hideously botched.

Adam was given the privilege of naming the woman God gave him. This implied, as it did with his naming the animals, his acceptance of authority. Godly authority is intended to build up rather than to pull down (see 2 Corinthians 10:8). Adam was also assigned the responsibility to care for, protect, provide for, cherish, and *husband* his wife.

She was made to be his helper, comforter, lover.

He was to initiate, she to respond.

But the roles were quickly reversed. Eve took the initiative in disobeying God by eating the fruit of the Tree of the Knowledge of Good and Evil, a fruit forbidden by the Lord because He had not created the man and the woman to sustain the terrible burden of such knowledge. Eve took the word of the serpent as more trustworthy than God's, and Adam went along with it.

She initiated. He responded. Sin, sorrow, and death were the result.

Note what happened when women took the lead in the following stories.

"Six months after receiving Christ as my Savior I found myself strongly attracted to a single man in my church. So I called up one of the pastors I was close to and asked him how I should handle it. I knew that there was a difference between the world's ways (the ways I had been living for twenty-three years) and God's ways.

"Oh, how I wish he had given me your advice, but instead, after my feelings had continued for a month, he told me I should let this young man know. Big mistake. *Three* other pastors at the church gave me the same advice, saying, 'If I were a single woman, I would . . .' But they are not women! Now I live with the consequences of a strained relationship with a man who I see quite often because we go to the same church and we have the same friends.

"Yuck! I wish I could move to the other side of the world! I need to say there were a few people who gave me your advice (as you can see, I talked to too many people, lacking discretion 'big time') but I could not hear them. Fortunately, the Lord is making this more clear to me. I am a lot more open to those 'old fashioned' ideas. Thank you for giving us young women a chance."

The author of a book with a title something like *Instant Rapport* appeared on a television interview. Although she gave her theories a more respectable name she was in fact lecturing women on how to flirt (as if the daughters of Eve lack that skill!). How many sensible women can swallow advice that tells them to "ascertain attraction strategy," use "representational" language ("when I see you I hear a voice inside me that makes me feel we could make it together"), and establish "sensory communication," which can be done by "mirroring," i.e., copying body movements. That women will flock to hear that sort of twaddle and solemnly gulp down such instructions should not surprise us, I suppose. As G. K. Chesterton observed, "When people stop believing in God they don't start believing in nothing—they'll believe in anything."

"I've been on a roller coaster since the student conference. I met a great guy. We really seemed to click, and I was greatly spellbound by his spiritual hunger—a man after God's own heart. We exchanged phone numbers and for three weeks I waited patiently. He never called. I saw him again at a meeting. He smiled, came over, and hugged me. I introduced him to my best friend who had heard so much about him she couldn't wait to meet him too.

"Something went wrong. He started talking to her much more than he talked to me. Then he took her out and I was devastated.

"I decided to call him, just as I would call any of my friends. We talked for hours. Then I asked him to go to a sorority social, just as friends. He understood and we had a terrific time. He kept saying he really wanted to spend more time with me and I agreed as long as he understood we were just friends. Then I asked him to the sorority formal. We went, and the next week he bought me a teddy bear, told me he 'liked' me, and I ended up telling him everything I had been feeling. . . .

"Then something strange happened. He stopped calling. Later he told me he was sorry for hurting me but he felt like this was God's will. Still wanted to be friends, said I could call him anytime. So I did, but the conversation was kinda awkward."

There were two more pages, revealing even greater confusion. Then, when I wrote for permission to print this letter, the lady responded with a sequel, granting permission to print this too.

"My prayer is that my story will help some woman not to make the same mistake I made. I did not heed the advice that your husband gave in his letter. [Something like, "Back off! The man's not really interested. He's using you."] I somehow rationalized and said things would be different. The result was one of the most heart-breaking semesters I've ever had. He kept saying things to make me think there was a future for us. Then suddenly he was interested in someone else again. That soon ended, and he was back to me, took me out, and I made the age-old mistake of associating physical intimacy with love. When he kissed me, I thought I had what I wanted at last! I was *very wrong*. I was completely devastated. . . .

"Thankfully we didn't end up together. . . .

"I have learned to be content in all circumstances, with or without someone, and have grown much closer to God. . . . I know He has great blessings in store for me if I keep following Him."

From another state, another letter, another girl, "second verse, same as the first!"

"I love (or think that I love) an incredible man of God. I was immediately attracted to him, not only for his physical appearance, but for his character and most importantly his faith-filled life. I could see the presence of the Lord in him. The weekend after the retreat I traveled home from college to make one of the seemingly fatal mistakes that you describe in your book. I came forward with my feelings."

Then followed a "friendship" that "intensified."

"Both he and I were initiating. . . . I struggled through the fall but in November I asked him where we stood. He told me he was attracted to me but was choosing not to have sexual feelings for me. The door was not totally closed, he said, but chances were good that his feelings would not change."

This hapless girl, torn to bits emotionally, hopeful for love, earnest about wanting to please God, suffers as do so many these days, in ways that I believe are unnecessary. The risks of falling in love are, of course, not new, but the loss of *form* in courtship is new. Nobody really knows how to behave. How much of her suffering might have been avoided if she had not come forward with her feelings in the first place. But I was thankful to find her making a wise choice in the end, as her last paragraph tells us.

"I have been trying to get rid of the feelings, hoping that our friendship could be platonic. Now, instead of praying that these feelings be taken away, I realize that this struggle to make the Lord the focus and center of my life is invaluable and that these feelings are not innately bad. What I do with them is the problem. . . . I have begun to feel that maybe I should simply withdraw totally from this relationship. I wonder if maybe I have let my feelings and preferences override the Lord's plan for me. I would like to be able to say, 'Lord, Your will be done.' But my passion seems to get in the way. My decision seems to be whether I should continue the relationship or pull out— either with or without an explanation—and then put my energy into dying to myself and relying completely on the Lord Jesus Christ."

"Thank you for reinforcing my already held belief in the need for men to initiate. Deep inside I have always felt bugged by eager females who take action into their own hands. To bear the thought of never knowing if *he* would have pursued *me* seems awful! Now, I will *wait.*"

"I am thirty years old and have been married to a most wonderful man for four years now. I attribute the success and joy of our relationship to my early Christian training by my parents, and most of all, to my exposure to [certain] books in my early twenties.

"When I met Dale I was so tempted to chase him—for it seemed he did not notice me for the longest time. For two years I was his friend and never let him know I had any feelings for him. I even had to stand by in silence as he dated my roommate for a few months. But the principles I learned from those books were ingrained in my heart and I determined that I wanted him ONLY if he fell in love with me on his own, with no external prompting. My internal struggle was intense, but I finally gave Dale up on the altar of my heart.

"When he did initiate a courtship with me I was more shocked than anyone. Later he told me that he was attracted to me because of the character, high standards, and self-respect he saw in me. During our courtship we maintained strict rules about physical contact, and the result is a marriage solidly built on trust and mutual respect. We have no regrets, no shame. Our relationship is so joyful!

"I know you receive many letters from those who received your advice too late. I thought you might like to hear from someone who received it at just the right time."

There are men who are delighted to have women come after them. They have hesitated to initiate for one reason or another, or perhaps had not even noticed the girl who noticed them. Letters of protest to the principle of a man's being created to be the initiator will not surprise me. I stand by the principle.

Reflections on "When Women Initiate"

- Study Genesis 1 and 2 to evaluate the ways in which the man and woman were alike (or "equal") and unlike.

- Does the physical difference between a man and a woman signal anything about initiation and reception? Does it mean anything beyond the physical?

- In the apostle Peter's exhortation to women (1 Peter 3:1–6) note particularly: "without words," "the unfading beauty of a gentle and quiet spirit." He is speaking, of course, to married women. Might these apply also to any woman who hopes for marriage?

12

No Courtship
Till after the Proposal

If we hope for what we do not yet have, we wait for it
patiently.

Romans 8:25

We also rejoice in our sufferings, because we know that
suffering produces perseverance; perseverance, character;
and character, hope. And hope does not disappoint us,
because God has poured out his love into our hearts by
the Holy Spirit, whom he has given us.

Romans 5:3–5

The trauma of unrequited love has been the story line of
many a famous novel. It was a personal drama for Dick Hillis,
missionary to China, even through the unfolding drama of
God's grace toward him in the Honan. He was in love with
a beautiful girl, and she was in love with his best friend.

Though his life was full of the many tasks and joys that are a missionary's, he was often plagued with emptiness. He had friendships with many of his Chinese countrymen, but he still felt a deep loneliness. His days bulged with activity, yet he longed for something more. He longed for Margaret Humphrey.

Frustration washed over him each time her name and face came to his mind. The beautiful dark-haired girl with hazel eyes and gentle smile was an ocean away and yet as present as the fur-lined parka he pulled on each day. He could not remove her from his thoughts. And to further complicate the matter, she was only vaguely aware of his existence.

He had been only a few months into his relationship with Jesus Christ when love hit him. But the object of his love was soon going steady with his best friend.

Dick could not simply give up and look for someone else. *Why search elsewhere when you have already found what you want?* his heart said. But what he wanted was outside his reach.

Yet she continued to fill his thoughts and his prayers.

In the last hours before Dick's boat sailed for China he had still refused to give up. He recruited a trusted friend to act as a benign spy.

"Write me every six months," he instructed his friend. "Just tell me how she is, what she's doing, and—well, if she's still going steady."

For four years the letters arrived from America. Time ticked by in six-month increments, carrying the monotonous toll of "situation status quo."

Dick often reminded himself that Jacob of the Old Testament waited seven years for his bride. He wondered if the same would be asked of him. He had loved her throughout his years at Bible school. Now after four years in China he could not stop loving her. Yet he wondered, *Have I made a mistake? Am I clinging to a wild dream?*

Promises and proverbs jumbled in his mind as he sought his Bible for guidance, some kind of assurance, hope maybe, that God would give him Margaret for his wife.

"Hope deferred maketh the heart sick," he read in Proverbs. And then, "He that spared not His own son . . . how shall He not also freely give us all things?"

He was sure she was God's choice for him. Time could not erase her face from his mind, nor her name from his lips. His loneliness for her did not subside even in the face of his demanding work among the Honan's masses.

He ached for the companionship of Margaret Humphrey, for the joy of private jokes and whispered words, for the bliss of holding her in his arms. Yet even as he dreamed of her, reality infringed on his mind: She had probably given him little or no thought since he left for China.

It was a very hot summer day when the Chinese postman handed him another "spy" letter. Dick opened it with very little anticipation. He knew by heart what it had to say. But as his eyes scanned the words, he suddenly caught his breath.

"They are no longer going together. Margaret feels that God wants her to serve in China. She has already applied to the China Inland Mission . . . has been accepted . . . and will sail in six months."

Before he reached the last sentence his legs felt like over-cooked Chinese noodles. He dropped to his knees and prayed, "Thank you, God! If you will only get her safely to Shanghai, I'll do the rest!"

Then suddenly he remembered, *I have no reason to believe that she is interested in me!* And he asked himself, *What am I going to do? I can't go to Shanghai and meet her. I can't just leave my work and travel hundreds of miles to woo a girl I haven't seen for four years. What would the mission think? O Lord, I will need your help in this matter even after she arrives in Shanghai!*

He had no choice but to make his first move by letter. "Faint heart never won fair lady" goes the saying. So he mustered all his courage and put his heart in a letter that went something like this:

> For years I have loved you. I have prayed for you and want you to be my wife. You have not seen me for nearly five years, but we did know each other pretty well for the years we were in Bible school. You will say you can't accept my proposal without courtship. I have to answer that in our circumstances there can be no courtship until you have accepted my proposal. This is hard, I know, but it looks as if your decision must be based on God's will for your life. It is easy for me to believe that you are God's will for *my* life as I have already admitted my deep love for you. For you it is a much bigger problem, so I will gladly give you six months to answer me. This allows you time to really pray. God will show you His will, I know.
>
> Before I close, let me ask you a question. Did you come to China because you loved the Chinese or because you were sure this was God's will for you? I know your answer—you came because you knew it was His will. Knowing this, you are confident that He will give you His love for the Chinese. Will you, dear, let me relate this same clear logic to your decision? If it is His will for you to be my wife, then will He not give you a love for me? Margaret, I will be praying every day—many times every day—because I love you.

Margaret Humphrey arrived in Shanghai in October 1936. She had expected strange emotions and confusing experiences upon her arrival in a foreign country. The mission orientation classes had tried to prepare her for those. But nothing could have prepared her for the confused state of her feelings when she opened the letter that was waiting for her at the mission headquarters the day she arrived.

She stared at the signature at the bottom of the letter. *Dick Hillis.* Her forehead creased in puzzlement. She remembered him from her Bible institute days as a good-looking young man known for his outgoing personality and unusual energy.

"But I haven't given him more than a fleeting thought since he left for China!" she mused in amazement. Letting her mind rove back over the years she recalled his more than passing interest in her during their years together at Biola.

But even then, she thought, *I felt nothing more than friendship toward him.* And now this—a marriage proposal! She was baffled and more than a little shocked.

Margaret had had her share of marriage proposals in recent years. But she had refused to let anything or anyone interfere with her desire to serve God as a missionary in China. After graduation from Biola, she attended the University of Washington. Then she applied to and was accepted by the China Inland Mission.

Now she arrived in China full of confidence that she was finally embarking on her life's work. But her confidence changed into confusion as she regarded the letter from Dick Hillis. *What am I going to do?* she asked herself. *What am I going to do?*

In honesty she had to say she did not love him. She admired him and had enjoyed his company on the few occasions they had been together. But after four years in China he could be a completely different person. And, like any other young woman, she had her own dreams of some day experiencing "great love." Was she to lay that aside in order to marry a man who was, in many ways, a stranger to her?

She could make no decision at the moment. She needed time. Would six months be enough, she wondered, to determine if this man she had not seen for so long was the man God had chosen to be her husband?

"Lord," she prayed, "You have guided me this far. I will trust You to lead me into the decision that will glorify You!"

Margaret was determined to tell no one about the marriage proposal she had received from the young missionary living in the Honan province. She would pray about it alone and wait to see the direction God would lead.

On one of her first days in Shanghai, a missionary lady invited her to tea, and for no apparent reason, the conversation turned toward the subject of marriage.

"I met my husband only once," the veteran missionary told Margaret, "before he proposed to me. I prayed about it and felt God was telling me to accept."

Margaret sat forward on her seat, her attention riveted on the woman whose face was filled with peaceful joy.

"We were married not long after that," she continued. "God has blessed our marriage with true love that has grown deeper through the years."

Margaret wondered at the time why she had been selected to hear this story of the woman's unusual marriage. She was soon treated to another moment that caused her to wonder. She paid a visit to one of her former Biola professors who was teaching in China for a year.

"Margaret," the woman said, "I have been praying for quite some time that God will bring you and Dick Hillis together."

Margaret was shocked. No one knew of the letter containing the proposal. No one knew of the searching that was going on in her mind as she daily prayed and considered what God would have her do about Dick Hillis.

The prayers of this saintly woman are usually answered, she thought, and trepidation filled her.

Within a few short days the mission sent Margaret to the China Inland Mission's Women's Language School in the city of Yangchow. She was busy from dawn to late evening, studying the language, becoming acquainted with China's complex culture, and learning to know her missionary classmates. She had little time to do more than daily pray about Dick's proposal and carry on a weekly correspondence with him.

Through his letters she came to know him as a direct and definitely appealing young man. She was soon looking forward to his letters and often found herself storing up bits and pieces of her life that she wanted to send to him in her next letter.

In March she learned that she could not put her decision off much longer. The mission director was due to arrive soon to appoint each of the new missionaries to their stations. They would be scattered all over China. Unless she told the director that she had future plans including a certain young missionary in Honan, Margaret might find herself sent to a distant southwestern or northwestern province for a seven-year term. That would no doubt rule out any possibility of marriage to Dick.

Yet still she wrestled alone with the question. How was she to decide God's will? She recalled God's guidance in the past, how He had used little signs along the way to lead her to Biola, to the University of Washington, and then to China. Did it mean something that God had called her to the same country as Dick, to the same mission organization, and that Dick had waited for her all these years?

She prayed and waited, and as the six months came to an end, she knew she had come to a decision. A deep inner assurance filled her. She knew that marriage to Dick Hillis was God's plan for her life. There could be no doubting it. She was certain.

Before Dick received her letter saying yes, she told the mission director God wanted her to go to the Honan province and become Mrs. Dick Hillis.

Though the decision was made, and though she could not doubt the rightness of that decision, there was a measure of fear in her mind.

"Lord, I'm not afraid of doing Your will," she confided in her prayers, "but I am afraid of the unknown. And so much of my future husband is unknown to me."*

Dick's letters did much to remove the fear from Margaret's mind. They were full of all the love and exuberance of a young bridegroom-to-be. And Margaret began to sense a responsive love for him growing in her own heart once she said yes to God.

The wedding plans took form through the letters that traveled between them. The ceremony was scheduled to take place in Hankow, central China, in six months.

Six months! Dick thought. *It's too long.* And yet, six months didn't seem so long compared to the six years he had already waited for the love of the woman of his dreams.

* Jan Winebrenner, *Steel in His Soul* (Colorado Springs: OC International). Used by permission.

Reflections on "No Courtship Till after the Proposal"

- Does a proposal that precedes a courtship seem preposterous? What "clear logic" helped to convince this couple that it could be just what God was directing them to do?

- When a decision has been made after prayer and clear guidance, should it surprise us that confidence can change to confusion? What did Margaret do when this happened?

- In what ways was the will of God made known to this couple? Were there any voices, visions, pillars of fire, or handwriting on the wall?

- What might we learn of God's usual methods of guidance?

13

Men with the Courage to Love

Be on your guard; stand firm in the faith; be men of courage;
be strong.

1 Corinthians 16:13

Dick Hillis is a man of faith and courage, a man whose
heart is ruled by God. His love for Margaret was deep, constant, and agonizing, yet he entrusted that love to his Father
and proceeded single-heartedly to do the work given him
to do. Where did he get that kind of strength? From the
same source as the knight of whom it was said,

> His strength was as the strength of ten
> Because his heart was pure.

A pure heart is a single heart, not divided. A pure heart
wills what God wills, no matter what the cost. Strength of
will is to will *against* oneself, to say, "Not my will—Thine."

Anthony Trollope wrote, "They say that faint heart never won fair lady; it is amazing to me how fair ladies are won, so faint are often men's hearts."

If that was true in 1854, what shall we say of the faintness of men's hearts today? Perhaps we should not be surprised. An article in the *Wall Street Journal* points out that liberal certitudes about the proper relations between the sexes have produced an absolutely contrary reality to that which was anticipated. Who in the nineteen fifties and sixties dreamed of handing out condoms to high school students, of discovering an epidemic of a fatal venereal disease, of an appalling upsurge in homosexuality and lesbianism? Who would have imagined movies about sexual aggression in which men engage in serial murders of women and women kill men to protest sexual harassment? And this is entertainment?

> "Repressions" and "taboos" are gone, and free sex seems to be generating anxiety and anger and misery without end. A century of liberal social thought about men, women, and sex lies in ruins about us.
>
> Irving Kristol, *Wall Street Journal,* May 12, 1992

Kristol goes on to relate the history of "ladies and gentlemen," a concept understood in Shakespeare's day to refer to a tiny minority of aristocrats. A "bold Victorian invention" extended the category to enable all women potentially to enter it, by education and self-improvement. A middle-class or lower-class man could become a gentleman by treating ladies with respect, remembering, for example, to stand when a lady entered the room, or to offer a seat to a lady on a bus or train. Such little acts of deference are considered incomprehensible, even indefensible, to our younger, more "liberated" generations, as illustrated by a student's angry response to a male professor's opening the door for her.

The ladies-and-gentlemen relationship, once a happy arrangement acceptable to both sexes, has been discarded. We are now equal, which in the feminist vocabulary is synonymous with interchangeable, except, for example, when they protest that the only woman student in a military academy should not be required to have her head shaved. The changes this outrageous concept has wrought in the lives of both men and women are so shocking, so destabilizing, that no one knows how to cope. Individual autonomy—"I gotta be me," "gotta do my own thing"—is called freedom, but in reality it is a new kind of bondage, bringing confusion and disorientation.

My husband and I were asked for advice by a young man who described to us the woman he was interested in and had, in fact, been dating for more than two years. She was a dedicated Christian, attractive, fun to be with, et cetera, et cetera. In fact, "she's everything I want in a wife."

"Are you engaged?" we asked.

"Oh no—I can't do *that!*"

"You've been dating for more than two years and haven't proposed? Why?"

"Well, because I don't know how she feels." (Must the lady put all her cards on the table first?)

"I'll tell you how to find out—real fast," said Lars.

"How?"

"Ask her to marry you. She'll tell you how she feels!"

But how blunt! And how simple! Aren't we supposed to struggle along for years, experiment, share feelings, make sure every aspect of both personalities matches perfectly?

A gentleman wants to win the lady. A lady wants to be won by wooing. Both terms—winning and wooing—have gotten lost in the shuffle. Many women have no desire to be thought of as ladies, having been persuaded there is something invidious about that category. Men tiptoe lest they be accused of male chauvinism or sexual harassment.

If both sexes have equal rights nobody knows what they are.

"'Rights' seems to be the only acceptable language today," says Kristol. "The trouble with this rhetoric is that it creates confusion. It tells men that they are to treat women with respect and circumspection—but without explaining why women's sexual identity merits such treatment."

"Is it any wonder students don't date?" asks John Mallon of Boston University.

> The sexual revolution has killed romance. A couple walking hand in hand on campus is an unusual sight. I have a feeling that many starchy old professors who once harrumphed at that sort of thing now secretly long to see it.
>
> One year the girls complained that the boys never asked them out. The next year the boys complained that the girls wouldn't go out with them—indeed, were astonished at being asked and needed to have it explained to them.

When tradition and standards are thrown to the winds it is no wonder men's hearts are faint, and fair ladies take the initiative or retire in confusion. The absence of models to emulate makes the approach to marriage simply too stressful.

If the sexual revolution has killed romance, in the sense in which Mallon uses the word, there is another sense in which it has perverted the meaning of the word. If sexual activity is readily available without any commitment whatever, and has, in the minds of many, no particular connection with *love*, then love in its true sense is degraded to an elusive something called *romance*, which either happens or doesn't happen. If it doesn't happen, two people who might have made a very happy marriage convince themselves that the absence of the requisite feelings prohibits their future happiness. If romance happens, and a marriage is built on that indefinable happening, the result

95

may be great disillusionment because after a few weeks or months it may not be happening anymore.

"I'm dating a wonderful guy, he's ready for engagement. He has qualities I want in a husband, I enjoy being with him, but I don't feel like I'm in love with him. I just don't have overwhelming feelings of emotion for him. How important *are* those feelings? I'm over thirty. Perhaps I have idealized what I think it should be like, how I should feel. Is liking him and making an intellectual decision to marry enough?"

Another way of putting the question came from someone else. "Should you marry someone who loves you deeply or should you marry someone you love deeply? I don't feel 'head over heels' about him. I can't say I love him, so I feel hypocritical, not totally honest."

C. S. Lewis defines "falling in love" as similar to the explosion that starts the engine. Must one wait for the explosion? *Being-in-love* is a feeling. Real love goes far beyond feeling. The great Love Chapter in the Bible, 1 Corinthians 13, describes what God calls love. It will be seen that romantic feelings, far from being prerequisite, have nothing to do with it.

> This love of which I speak is slow to lose patience—it looks for a way of being constructive. It is not possessive: it is neither anxious to impress nor does it cherish inflated ideas of its own importance.
>
> Love has good manners and does not pursue selfish advantage. It is not touchy. It does not keep account of evil or gloat over the wickedness of other people. On the contrary, it is glad with all good men when truth prevails.
>
> Love knows no limit to its endurance, no end to its trust, no fading of its hope; it can outlast anything. It is, in fact, the one thing that still stands when all else has fallen.
>
> 1 Corinthians 13:4–8 *Phillips*

Reflections on "Men with the Courage to Love"

- Consider the supreme aim of Dick Hillis. Ask yourself, What is mine?
- Are men afraid of women?
- Is a faint heart one that is not yet sure of its God?
- "Now that you have purified yourselves by obeying the truth so that you have sincere love for your brothers, love one another deeply, from the heart" [some early manuscripts have "from a pure heart"] (1 Peter 1:22). Is there an important clue here?

14

Hook 'Em
and Throw 'Em Back

Brothers, as an example of patience in the face of suffering, take the prophets who spoke in the name of the Lord.
As you know, we consider blessed those who have perse-
vered. You have heard of Job's perseverance and have seen
what the Lord finally brought about. The Lord is full of
compassion and mercy.

Above all, my brothers, do not swear—not by heaven
or by earth or by anything else. Let your "Yes" be yes and
your "No," no, or you will be condemned.

James 5:10–12

The Southwell Litany for the Personal Life contains this
prayer.

From moral weakness of spirit; from timidity; from hesitation; from fear of men and dread of responsibility,
strengthen us with courage to speak the truth in love and

self-control; and alike from the weakness of hasty violence and weakness of moral cowardice,
  Save us and help us, we humbly beseech Thee, O Lord.
From weakness of judgment; from the indecision that can make no choice; from the irresolution that carries no choice into act; and from losing opportunities to serve Thee,
  Save us and help us, we humbly beseech Thee, O Lord.

(Cincinnati: Forward Movement Publications)

Weakness of judgment and the indecision that can make no choice are painfully evident in the following accounts.

"I was recently in a correspondence with a neat Christian guy while I was on a short-term mission overseas. He was in the States, waiting for my return. He sent me photos of his family and care packages, and at the end of my term he wanted me to visit his parents who are missionaries. I was eager to meet them since his weekly letters to me had spoken so highly of them and had shown that his parents were equally eager to meet me. I guess my first clue that he wasn't so sure about me should have been his nervousness about the thought of my return. Perhaps it was only then that he realized that he'd been communicating more to me than he wanted to. He'd obviously communicated the wrong thing to his parents too, as I was treated very specially when I visited them. While at their home, I received a letter from him stating that he was 'bumping into' another girl all over town, and they were having wonderful times together.

"His welcome home kiss just confused me all the more as I asked him where things stood. He said he'd rather spend time with the other girl. Living the past two years overseas, I thought I could handle cross-cultural communication, but I think that men and women are the most difficult cultural gulf to cross! The idea that he didn't realize what he was communicating to me with gifts of jewelry and clothes is almost ridiculous to me. I'm not bitter.

I can see the good of this situation, and I praise God that I am no longer in a relationship with someone like this."

Another letter.

"We decided to just be friends, but after a few times of seeing each other, he popped the question. I was excited, but said we'd have to spend more time together. A few minutes later he kissed me and I forgot everything. It was the most beautiful kiss I'd ever experienced.

"We saw each other once a week for two and a half years, but just to get attention I began seeing someone else. He liked me so much. Then my sweetheart moved to town and I told him about Number Two. I saw both of them for three months, got more physical with Number One, and suddenly he began to act differently, so I suggested a wedding. Well, he agreed, and we went to counseling at the church. He was so ornery he really got into it with the minister.

"I decided to call it off. We continued seeing each other. He begs me to marry him. I agreed, set date, then in a few days I broke it off again. He moved out of town and was seeing someone else, but I started contemplating marriage again, then lo & behold I start seeing someone else.

"I fell hopelessly in love with Number Three but when I told him about Number Two he suggested we be just friends but that didn't work. I might tell you I'm divorced, middle-aged, have been looking for a man for fifteen years. It seems like they're all running the other way. I gradually stopped chasing. I prayed, asked God to have me married right away. Seemed like a good prayer, I felt better. Writing this letter I see what a desperate chase I've had without much progress. How does God's plan work in this case?"

Poor lady. This chaotic tale ends with her telling me she had read *Passion and Purity,* which had obviously been no help at all. She appears to be ignorant of the prerequisites for grasping the plan of God, which are clearly laid out in Romans 12:1–2.

> Offer your bodies as living sacrifices, holy and pleasing to God—this is your spiritual act of worship. Do not conform any longer to the pattern of this world, but be transformed by the renewing of your mind. Then you will be able to test and approve what God's will is—his good, pleasing, and perfect will.

One man told me of making a great effort to be faithful and "as a result" has given his girlfriend "a really rough time." They have broken up and gotten back together no less than four times and have finally broken the engagement. "But this time we *both* understand why and both are willingly seeking God's will in our lives. . . . We have learned how destructive physical intimacy can be. How *sinful*, too."

Another told a woman he wanted to spend the rest of his life with her. She believed him. He asked her to tell her parents and arrange for him to meet them. She did. He decided then that something was missing. He loved her spirituality, he said, her values, her love for him. All that was just great, but . . .

The man faded out of the picture.

"I'm angry, hurt, rejected, betrayed," she wrote. "Thank you for saying that trusting God with your lovelife is a rigorous daily exercise of faith."

We are called to *live* by faith. Everything that happens, God's Word tells us, fits into a pattern for good to those who love Him. The more intimately we walk with Him, the more faithfully we trust His promises and keep His commandments, the simpler and the happier we will be. Life will "uncomplicate" itself.

My father was a dedicated trout fisherman, spending the most blissful days of his life wading in the crystalline lakes of the White Mountains of New Hampshire, wearing hip boots and casting his delicate, hand-tied flies, or creeping along the wooded brink of some tiny brook where the beautiful and elusive "natives" might lurk in the shadows of a rocky pool. Two of my brothers caught his passion and loved to accompany him on these often futile expeditions. The area, having been discovered by almost every fisherman north of Baltimore, had been pretty well fished out, so the trout were hard to come by. Dave and Jim had fun sometimes catching "suckers," large, slow bottom fish that didn't begin to measure up to trout either in fight or flavor. They would hook them for the fun of it and throw them back. This struck me as cruel. They assured me the fish didn't mind. It was a sort of game for fish and fisherman.

One day I had lunch with a young woman who poured out her story, a sadly familiar one. When she got to this part I began to think about those fishing trips: "So our relationship grew. He's really a godly man. I found in him everything I've always wanted in a husband. He finally took me out for dinner to a really nice place. We hadn't *dated* a whole lot, exactly, we'd just spent a lot of time together—*quality* time, you know? Anyway, this really nice dinner. I was hyped. Maybe this would be it.

"He told me I was everything he'd ever wanted in a wife. Said he'd never loved anybody the way he loved me. We really did *care* about each other. I mean, our relationship was—well, it was very *special*, to both of us. Or—well, *I* thought it was, and he certainly gave me the impression that he thought so too.

"But then . . ."

I had no trouble filling in the rest of the story. I couldn't help wondering how often he'd gone fishing just for fun, how many he'd hooked and thrown back, treated like poor suckers, not as the beauties he was looking for. Suckers aren't good for much, but they're fun to hook and—oh well, it doesn't hurt them.

I have seen suckers with the scars of old hooks.

From moral weakness of spirit; from timidity; from hesitation; from fear of men and dread of responsibility. . . .

From weakness of judgment; from the indecision that can make no choice; from the irresolution that carries no choice into act. . . .

Save us and help us, we humbly beseech Thee, O Lord.

Reflections on "Hook 'Em and Throw 'Em Back"

- Perhaps we might ponder the causes of chaos in these stories, that we may avoid them.
- Humility, obedience, repentance, and the fear of the Lord put us in a position to be instructed in the way He chooses for us. Memorize Psalm 25:9–12.
- Pray the quotation from the Southwell Litany. And remember the Lord is our *Helper!* Do not despair!

15

God Chooses the Weak

I will boast all the more gladly about my weaknesses, so that Christ's power may rest on me. That is why, for Christ's sake, I delight in weaknesses, in insults, in hardships, in persecutions, in difficulties. For when I am weak, then I am strong.

2 Corinthians 12:9–10

Hudson Taylor was a physician and the founder of the China Inland Mission, now known as Overseas Missionary Fellowship. He was a man greatly revered in his time and perhaps even more so after his death. It is not hard to understand why, when a man has been a powerful instrument in the hand of God, his weaknesses may surprise us. We ought not to be surprised. A reading of the biographies in the Bible confirms the fact that the men God chooses to do mighty things are without exception fallible men.

I include Taylor's vacillations in the hope that men and women who have discovered the same weakness in themselves will be encouraged to look to the faithful God who views with mercy our seemingly irremediable confusions. He is still at work in the midst of them, making up for us our own undoings, restoring the years that the locust has eaten.

Hudson Taylor, son of a chemist who was also a Methodist preacher in a Yorkshire mining town, fell in love while still in his teens with a young music teacher, Miss Vaughan. He did not declare his love.

"What can I do?" he wrote to his sister Amelia on November 11, 1850. "I know I love her. To go to China without her would make the world a blank." But he felt he could not expect the girl to share the poverty he anticipated as a missionary, and she had no idea of going to China. They were in each other's company from time to time and came to an "understanding"—they would be married. Privately, however, each felt sure he could change the other's mind. *He* would see to it that she went to China. *She* would overcome Hudson's absurd ambition. Neither succeeded. Her refusal made him "as wretched as heart could wish," but he was comforted in thinking of the love of God, which "thoroughly softened and humbled me."

Yet he could not relinquish her. In 1853 he made another effort to persuade her to marry him, in spite of his recognition of her unsuitability in outlook, constitution, and training. This time he was accepted, but a few weeks later he was writing to his sister, "I know I loved her and she says she loved me. But I know she does not love me as she did. . . . I fear it will have to be broken off. O do pray for me and write soon."

Miss Vaughan's father settled the matter by declaring that he would never consent to her going to China, so the engagement was broken by mutual agreement. During the engagement another friend, Elizabeth Sissons, used to say that she loved Hudson. She was there to console the rejected lover and made him a present of sketches. Upon his leaving England he gave her a brooch to remember him by.

Hudson Taylor, the sole passenger on the sailing vessel *Dumfries*, left Liverpool on September 19, 1853, "cheerful, boyish, and small," aged twenty-one. Twenty-three weeks later he landed in Shanghai, "a tedious voyage which the crew kindly laid to my account as they did every storm or calm or headwind or current, saying that ministers and missionaries generally caused a vessel to be lost."

He was not long in Shanghai before he felt "forlorn, miserable, and homesick." It is not surprising that his loneliness during that first year in China tempted him to self-pity. Even his sister did not write as often as he thought she should. He longed for a wife.

"I am glad to hear any news of Miss Vaughan you may have. She may get a richer and a handsomer husband but I question whether she will get one more devoted than I should have been. But I see she is not fit for a missionary's wife. It is very improbable that I shall ever meet with one here—the Americans do not very favorably impress me—perhaps that may be because I do not know them well enough. I feel that any soul that I could talk to of *our* country, *our* friends, would be an invaluable friend and a *good* wife. One who would sympathize with me and assist me in my labour would be an inestimable prize."

His thoughts turned again to Elizabeth Sissons and after some months he wrote to her, asking for a lock of her hair. She sent it in January, 1855, and after painting for her a rosy picture of life in China he wrote a formal proposal of marriage. Still he had secret misgivings—God had called him to the interior, while he felt that marrying Elizabeth would necessitate his remaining at the coast. Yet, surely, things would work out. Miss Sissons agreed to marry him, but her father thought it best that they wait. Taylor was willing to wait on God and trust Him.

In December 1855, Elizabeth wrote that she feared she did not love him. It was a knock-down blow, coming just at the time he had been thrown out of Tsungming, and "between one thing and another I was quite knocked down and had scarcely heart to read my other letters." He sent a long reply, "to plead my cause and that of the heathen," but the affair dragged on, more and more one-sided.

"I don't know what I shall do if I get an unfavorable letter this mail," he wrote to his mother on May 30. I sometimes feel as if it would be *more* than I could bear and would quite break me down. But I know it is wrong to give way to such feelings, that does not make it easier to avoid them." And again, "There is something in my nature that seems as if it must have love and sympathy."

> Hudson's career had shown his compulsion for love. His muddled attempts to end loneliness had led him to make offers which, if accepted, would have snuffed out the flame of his pioneering zeal. His existence cried aloud to be organized, to be understood: his natural impatience made him flounder about trying to construct a partnership which could come only as a gift.
>
> John C. Pollock, *Hudson Taylor and Maria*
> (New York: McGraw Hill, 1962)

He persisted in hoping for an affirmative. He wrote to Amelia that if there were no Elizabeth, bachelorhood would be the best choice, but "with Liz there can be no two opinions, *she* is *such* a treasure."

He went so far as to contemplate a return to England, since her father had said he would permit the marriage if his daughter were to remain there. That thought, however, seemed to put a "blight" on his prayer life.

A missionary lady in whom Hudson had confided mentioned Maria Dyer, who was working at a mission school in Ningpo. He remembered her as "a good-looking girl, despite the slightest cast of the eye." She was reputed to be devoted to her calling, the second best Chinese speaker in the community, and had turned down two other suitors. Doubts assailed him: How could he provide, for a woman of her social standing, the European lifestyle to which she was accustomed?

But during the ensuing months he was disturbed to discover strange feelings for Maria, unlike any he had felt for the Misses Vaughan and Sissons. He had an "attachment" for her, and "though unable to repress it, I strove to confine the knowledge of it to my own bosom."

Some months before, Maria had written about Hudson Taylor to her brother: "I met a gentleman and, I cannot say I loved him at once, but I felt interested in him and could not forget him. I saw him from time to time and still this interest continued. I had no good reason to think it was reciprocated, he was very unobtrusive and never made any advances." She took the matter to the Lord and then, early in January 1857 spoke to an older lady about her feelings. The lady discouraged her from hoping, having seen no evidence herself that Hudson was interested in Maria, "and remarked that it was a dreadful thing to love without the love being returned."

When the Anglo-Chinese war began, Hudson was asked to escort women and children from Ningpo to Shanghai. Maria remained, with several other missionaries, but waved good-bye to the steamer and wrote, "Before he left, I had some little reason, perhaps, to think that he might be interested in me, but I thought I had better not be too sanguine. I still continued to make the subject a matter of prayer."

Hudson wrote, "[My] state of feeling was one of great anxiety and pain. . . . Still I did not move in the matter, and in the latter part of January went up to Shanghai, making it a matter of prayer as before."

No wonder he experienced great anxiety and pain—all during January and February he considered himself bound to Elizabeth if she accepted his open offer, but she would not write. He began to wonder if he had protracted the correspondence too long yet felt he could not afford to lose her and was still willing to wait. He mentioned her often in his letters home but said not a word about Maria, though he thought her "a dear, sweet creature, has all the good points of Miss S., and many more too. She is a precious treasure, one of sterling worth and possessed with an untiring zeal for the good of this poor people. She is a *lady* too." While the cast of her eye disturbed him a little, it was now becoming dear to him because it made him feel that perhaps it gave him a chance to win her.

At long last, in mid-April, Miss Sissons wrote a letter that enabled him honorably to close the correspondence. "I have quite dismissed the matter as a settled question. I am thankful it has been ordered as it has."

It was certainly fortunate for him that the question was settled, for in March he had actually sent a proposal to Maria, which she received on April 8.

This was for both of them the beginnings of long travail—how to get a letter to her without going through the redoubtable Miss Aldersey, who, while not Maria's legal guardian, had been headmistress of the school where Maria and her sister were teaching. Taylor enclosed his proposal in a letter to a fellow missionary, Mr. Gough, who was very sympathetic and could be trusted with a confidence. He gave Hudson's letter to his wife, who sent a servant to Maria's classroom with a message that Mrs. Gough wished to see her. She begged Maria not to send a refusal. Maria did not recognize the handwriting but guessed the contents, and fearing it was from a suitor whom she had already rejected, slipped the letter into her satchel and returned to class.

"When school was over I retired to my room. Before opening the letters I prayed over them. I had a sort of hope that they might be from Mr. Taylor but I could not think that they were—that was not likely. . . . It seemed that my prayers were indeed answered, he asked me to consent to an engagement to him. He begged me not to send him a hasty refusal which he intimated would cause him the intensest anguish, and concluded by expressing the hope that ere long all his doubts and fears would be removed and his fondest hopes realized. He signed himself my most sincerely and affectionately James Hudson Taylor."

Next day she called on Miss Aldersey who said, "I presume you would not think of accepting him?" and proceeded to detail the reasons why to do so would be unthinkable: Mr. Taylor was a poor, unconnected Nobody, presumptuous, not a gentleman, without education, without position, a ranter, a canting Plymouth Brother, did not keep the Sabbath, was connected with "a *most* peculiar missionary" (a man named Burns), was short and Maria was tall, and—"*and*, he wears Chinese clothes!"

She then proceeded to dictate Maria's reply, a categorical refusal that was God's direction and her plain duty. She regarded Mr. Taylor as a brother in Jesus and requested that he never refer to the subject again. With Miss Aldersey standing over her shoulder Maria wrote as she was told.

Maria loved Hudson, dreamed of him, his blue eyes, his love for the Chinese, his devotion to Christ, his merry nature, his love of music. The Chinese dress did give her pause but she trusted his judgment—"it must be the right thing to do."

Hudson, suspecting that the hindrance was Miss Aldersey, went to see her in July. She was unbudgeable. Months of agony ensued, exacerbated for Maria because she had truly loved and admired Miss Aldersey. Maria and Hudson would occasionally find themselves in the same room, but not a word or even a look could be exchanged. The missionaries took sides, and even Maria's sister opposed the match because of Miss Aldersey's disapproval. Later an interview was arranged, with Mrs. Bausum present at Maria's request. The three prayed together for God's will.

One fellow missionary refused even to recognize Taylor as a Christian, instructed his wife to "cut him dead" (to treat him as though he did not exist), and said that a man acting as Mr. Taylor "ought to be horsewhipped." Maria was called fanatical, indecent, and weak-minded.

At last, on November 14, 1857, a meeting was arranged through an American missionary couple who had been in no way involved in the in-fighting. They invited Maria to their home. Hudson was there, his eye on the door. When it opened, she was in his arms.

"The result," wrote Hudson, "was that we were engaged whether the guardians' answer was favorable or otherwise. . . . I was not long engaged without trying to make up for the number of kisses I *ought* to have had these last few months."

Notwithstanding the implacable opposition of some, Hudson Taylor and Maria Dyer were married at last, on January 20, 1858.

Reflections on "God Chooses the Weak"

- Review this sequence:
  teenager falls in love with Miss Vaughan.
  She has no interest in missions.
  He thinks he'll change her mind.
  Her father refuses consent.
  Lonely, he begins to dwell on two possibilities—
      Miss Vaughan and Miss Sissons.
  In spite of uncertainties, he proposes to Miss Sissons.
  Discouragement—she doesn't love him.
  He *must* have love and sympathy.
  Impatience.
  He has "strange feelings for Maria."
  He develops an "attachment" while still bound to
      Miss Sissons.

Maria humbly submits to authority. Later she felt she must ignore authority in order to obey the Lord.

- Feeling inadequate? Unqualified to serve the Lord? Fearful about the matter of marriage? "God chose the foolish things of the world to shame the wise; God chose the weak things of the world to shame the strong. He chose the lowly things of this world and the despised things—and the things that are not—to nullify the things that are, so that no one may boast before him" (1 Cor. 1:27–29).

- Think of some of the great characters of the Bible who told God how unqualified they were, e.g., Moses (Exodus 3), Gideon (Judges 6), and others. What mattered was not who they were but who God is.

- "The Lord God will help me; therefore shall I not be confounded: therefore have I set my face like a flint, and I know that I shall not be ashamed" (Isa. 50:7 KJV).

16

Hearts Are Breakable

The LORD is close to the brokenhearted
and saves those who are crushed in spirit.

Psalm 34:18

Hudson Taylor's story is evidence that he, like all the rest of us, was merely a clay pot—common stuff, flawed, fragile, yet, in God's skillful hands, useful—"to show that this all-surpassing power is from God and not from us" (2 Cor. 4:7).

Each revelation of our own weakness is God's call to us to learn of Him, to find grace to help in time of need, and to lay hold of His power to re-create, to redeem, to forgive, and to mend.

Hearts do break. The same hearts are breakable over and over again. Letters come from couples who were engaged or very nearly engaged. One of them suddenly informs the other that they must break it off. The reason given, one which is thought to obviate all argument and dry all tears: "It's the will of God."

This is in some cases an honest explanation. Perhaps one has come to a new place of surrender to the Lord and discovered that he or she has made a serious mistake. Sincere Christians make many a mistake, and surely it is better to rectify it than to proceed as though no mistake had been made. The engagement must come to an end. Better now than after the wedding.

There is another possibility. The person had not sought God from the beginning. He or she had entered into a relationship carelessly, with no thought of self-offering, prayer, or waiting for a word from God. It was self-willed and irresponsible. Was "the will of God" the real reason or was it perhaps a failure of courage, an attraction elsewhere, the impulse of one governed primarily by feelings, a willful breach of contract—in other words, merely the will of the breaker-upper himself/herself?

"All a man's ways seem right to him, but the LORD weighs the heart" (Prov. 21:2). Whatever the heart's true reason may have been, we can be sure that God is never the author of confusion.

"My fiancé told me we needed to break up 'temporarily' to refocus on God. This broke my heart, but I accepted it. Seven weeks later he says he doesn't love me, it's too much trouble to be with me, I take no pride in my body, I'm sloppy."

What, exactly, is a "temporary" break-up when a couple is already committed to marriage? What would they tell their friends—"Yes, we *were* engaged, but we're not engaged right now. Oh yes, we *are* going to get married, but we're *not* engaged"? And as for the overweight and sloppiness—did it happen quite suddenly, unnoticed earlier?

This man's next move, she tells me, was to come back and announce that she is definitely to be his mate, but he wants to "move back into the commitment *slowly*." How, exactly, does one do that? Would it not have been best to keep silent until he was prepared to commit himself fully? To commit means to give in *trust*, to put into charge or keeping. It is a deliberate act, a total handing over, a pledge to do something. Since the man has made up his mind definitely to marry the lady, he has *made* a commitment. How does one "move slowly" into a position already taken? A high diver may spend a long time studying the water beneath him. He may make many a tentative jump on the board, but there comes the moment of decision. He does not then move slowly. He is resolute. His muscles tighten. He springs into the air, giving himself to a no-turning-back commitment. He hits the water.

One more story of "the irresolution that carries no choice into act."

"I was convinced the first time I saw him that he was the man I'd marry. 'This is ridiculous,' I told myself, 'you've lost it.' But five days in a row I ran into him and was almost overcome with feeling. I did lots of crying. He went away and called me every day for three weeks. Then he cut back to every other day, but wrote me a letter every day. 'I knew the minute I saw you I wanted to marry you,' he said, and proposed to me on the phone. I said yes. A friend confirmed our decision. She said, 'The Lord told me you're getting married.' Our parents were in favor, so was the pastor. Three weeks later he broke it because he said he was confused and needed time to think, etc. Two days later we were back together, and three days after that he broke it again, and even said he didn't love me. After that he called every week. My efforts to comfort him caused more pain. Now he calls to ask how I'm doing. I tell him 'Fine.' He presses me and then I tell him the truth. He clams up."

What can we say to the many women who find themselves in such an indefinable position? We pray for wisdom, and for something to help their wounded souls. I confess I would like to give the young man in this case a hard shake, but of course I'm not given that opportunity.

Is there anywhere to turn but to Him who "heals the brokenhearted and binds up their wounds"? Broken hearts are not new to Him, and His power is limitless, for He is the one who numbers the stars and calls them all by name. Have you noticed those two verses in Psalm 147 that juxtapose God's concern for the wounded *and* His numbering and naming the stars? His compassion and His power are mentioned together that we might understand that the Lord of the Universe is not so preoccupied with the galaxies that He cannot stoop to minister to our sufferings. He is the One who is in sovereign control of our lives, and of every single thing that touches them. Nothing can pass through the fortress of His love.

He has a glorious purpose in permitting the heartbreak. We find many clues for this in Scripture, for example:

- that we may be shaped to the likeness of Christ (Rom. 8:29)
- that we may learn to trust (2 Cor. 1:8–9)
- that we may learn to obey (Ps. 119:67, 71)
- that we may bear fruit (John 15:2)
- that we may reach spiritual maturity (James 1:4)

Our sufferings are not for nothing. Never. However small they may be, we may see them as God's mercy in giving us the chance to unite them with His own sufferings. Christ suffered for our sins and we suffer because of the sins of others (and they suffer because of ours). There is a mystery here, far deeper than our understanding, but we may take it on faith, on the authority of the Word, and believe it will not go for nothing.

But let us never suppose that since God always knows how to work for good to those who love Him, the wrong we commit against them is not wrong. It was *evil* men who worked *evil* against the Son of God at Calvary. It was the worst thing that ever happened. Yet God transformed it into the best thing: our salvation.

A broken heart is an acceptable offering to God. He will never despise it. We do not know what unimagined good He can bring about through our simple offering. Christ was willing to be broken bread for the life of the world. He was poured out like wine. This means He accepted being ground like wheat and crushed like the grape. It was the hands of others who did the grinding and crushing. Our small hurts, so infinitely smaller than His, may yet be trustfully surrendered to His transforming work. The trial of faith is a thing worth much more than gold.

Reflections on "Hearts Are Breakable"

- A broken heart is a reminder of our only source of power.
- It is a revelation of our weakness.
- It is a call from God—to do what?
- It is an acceptable offering.
- For what reasons does God permit a heart to break?
- Think of reasons in addition to those suggested.

17

Commitment Phobia

Commit your way to the LORD:
  trust in him and he will do this:
He will make your righteousness shine like the dawn,
  the justice of your cause like the noonday sun.

Psalm 37:5–6

A song Rod Stewart sang gives truthful expression to an attitude common to many today.

> I don't want to challenge you,
> marry you, or remember you,
> I just wanna make love to you.

That's putting it bluntly. Love imposes obligations. *Making* love, in the minds of such men and women, is a form of recreation, a feeling that may last for a few minutes, even an hour. Nothing more is implied, although much more may be expected. It is a means of self-satisfaction. But to challenge? Marry? Or even remember? Ah, there's a Catch-22: responsibility. At that they break into a cold sweat.

What shall we say of a man who, on his first approach, offered a woman something she says she could not resist: unconditional love? A man ought to be careful of his words. "Set a guard over my mouth, O Lord; keep watch over the door of my lips," was the psalmist's prayer (Psalm 141:3).

He promised he'd never leave, always be faithful.

"Well, we broke up three times and got back together. . . .

"One day I knew God Himself was speaking to me. I cried and wanted to obey, but I did not. I continued in this relationship that was not pleasing to the Lord. I rationalized that it was o.k. because he is a Christian. However, he is not in any way walking in obedience to the Lord."

This ought to have given the lady pause. Was it not a clear sign from heaven? A true Christian seeks to obey. "We know that we have come to know him if we obey his commands. The man who says, 'I know him,' but does not do what he commands is a liar, and the truth is not in him" (1 John 2:3–4).

"Again I compromised," she continues, "and can attest: THE PRICE IS TOO HIGH.

"We are no longer seeing each other because of his great fear of commitment. Though he says he loves me, he doesn't feel 'at peace' about marrying me. He says you're supposed to be very happy about such a decision, and instead of great joy, he only feels great fear. Therefore, for the fifth time (yes, fifth, I'm embarrassed to say) he has made an exit, though this time it was at my suggestion because he was manifesting his fear again, and I could no longer handle it. (I can almost hear you say, 'About time!')"

To commit oneself to marriage is to give oneself in trust, to put one's life at the disposal of the other. It is, in fact, actually to *forfeit* rights and to consign oneself to the charge of another person. One who commits his way to the Lord also does just this. No one will do that who does not trust Him. Whom do we trust? On whose integrity, veracity, justice, or even faithful friendship can we rely? Am *I* worthy of another's trust? Am *I* a person in whom confidence can be reposed?

Commitment entails the acceptance of responsibility. It imposes a task and a trust. It is a promise to do something, a pledge to pursue a certain course. To love is to make a commitment. Merely to *make* love while refusing commitment is a purely selfish act, irresponsible, and finally destructive.

Another case of "commitment phobia" comes from a woman whose male friend has sought to keep tabs on her for years, surfacing every so often, dating her when it suited him, telling her she's a wonderful "friend," and leaving it at that. Her biological clock has been ticking away, dreams of husband, home, and family fading.

"I'll give you a little update on what's been happening. He called last month (first time in months), just 'wanted to chat.' It became pretty obvious early on that I could no longer be interested. He talked about his plans for spring break, work, etc. but there wasn't much to say. . . .

"And as for the other man I told you about, I don't know. He moves forward, then backward. So as to prevent emotional whiplash I'm just trying to be consistent in responding when he pursues, but not reacting to his fears or hesitations. He hasn't asked me out. I have never had such difficulty communicating verbally with anyone before, so I'm learning to listen—a lot! Why are men so hesitant to initiate? It baffles me.

"A friend asked me the other day, 'Do you feel a need to rescue the wimps?' I laughed. I don't think my motives are of a 'rescue' nature. I'm only frustrated that men are not being men. Elisabeth, I believe Satan has a stronghold that must be broken by obedience and prayer in the lives of these young men. When young men do not marry and multiply, new generations are not being produced to proclaim the gospel until Jesus comes again. When men are not men and women not women, the mystery of the distinctives of our sexes is lost. I believe we should see the image of God in those distinctives. The Christian community has begun to develop an attitude about the *family* of believers (brothers and sisters in Christ) that veils the wonder of being our Maker's handiwork. Potluck dinners and socials on Saturday evening allow for 'relationships' to develop but men never have to come out of their comfort zones. Women, on the other hand, can satisfy in a measure their inclination to nurture and care for others. The result—nobody needs to get married."

It is not only men who fear commitment. A missionary woman became engaged to a national in the country where she served. She broke the engagement, went home on furlough, met another man who was on his way to mission work; they became engaged. When he told her he was going to a different country she broke the engagement and wrote to ask me if I thought it would be best to go back to the first man. What could I say?

There is a strange notion of commitment popular today— that of openness and vulnerability. There is a place for that, but caution is needed. Is it wise, does the Scripture teach us, to "get deep" with each other in groups, share, spread out our real feelings in the marketplace, as it were, exposing what we claim is the "true self"? Others, it is thought, may then identify one's strengths and weaknesses so that one can "own" them. In another age this was the prerogative of spiritual directors (and properly so), but few of us today have that spiritual luxury.

A public emotional and spiritual strip-tease is not merely embarrassing (at least for the onlookers) but, it seems to me, dangerous and possibly wrong. To take one's emotions and needs quite simply to the foot of the cross and look unflinchingly at them there usually shows us what we need to know. God may give us a godly helper—a spiritual mother or father—who understands and knows how to pray. Let us be grateful for and pay close attention to what such a one says. But let us beware of group intimacies.

John Mallon relates commitment phobia to the present day "culture of pornography."

Most men in our society have grown up with the idea that any form of sexual activity, including promiscuity and masturbation, supported by soft-core pornography, is something good, something healthy. . . .

The man begins a fantasy sexual life in his early adolescence . . . with the use of soft-core pornography, such as Playboy magazines, gets a habit deeply ingrained in his psyche linking a false idea of female perfection with an ideal fantasy harem. None of the members of his fantasy harem has any qualms about his fantasizing about another woman, and even seem to approve, because that is all the woman's eyes in those photographs ever communicate. She is all approving, all understanding, and lovingly naked— for him. . . . No one gets hurt or jealous. Hence he is free always to search for that more perfect woman—each month. . . .

Now translate this mindset firmly formed, and deeply linked to this man's patterns of needs into the real world of real women and real love affairs. At first he is all hearts and flowers, candy, cards, presents, dinner and dancing, until she starts to like it and believes he really cares for her—and he does. But can he commit to just one? To her alone? Or is he always scanning the horizon for something (as opposed to someone) "better"? Is he capable of truly loving a woman or merely addicted to adolescent romantic fantasy linked to sexual gratification, which is now unquenchable by one woman? He will weep with sincere frustration that she can't tolerate his desire for more and others. He is accustomed to the unquestioning sweetness and acceptance of his paper harem, and genuinely can't understand himself. He feels no guilt over the sense that he is using this real live woman in the same way. She's fed up, he's in terror, facing more rejection, shame, and terrible loneliness, doesn't know what happened, and can't help himself. Such is the way of sin. . . .

A fantasy world of concubinage destroys one's ability to love, and creates a cynicism towards trust, which is obviously a necessary component of loving commitment. The so-called sexual revolution has liberated no one but rather has thrust us deeper into isolation and loneliness and cynicism. . . . Women have paid the highest and most conspicuous price, as they always do when sexual mores are loosened.

Reflections on "Commitment Phobia"

- Give examples of commitments we make other than to marriage. Are they frightening? Why or why not?
- What obligations does a commitment to another person—for example, the boss, a professor, one's parents—impose? Would the word *commitment* be defined differently for each obligation?
- Since none of us are invulnerable what do people mean by the willingness to be vulnerable?
- Think about Mallon's analysis of commitment phobia. Perhaps you can cite other causes.
- Fear God and fear nothing else.

18

At Any Cost

They were put to death by the sword. . . . The world was
not worthy of them. . . . These were all commended for
their faith, yet none of them received what had been promised. God had planned something better for us so that only
together with us would they be made perfect.

Hebrews 11:37–40

For the Christian, an understanding of commitment must
come first of all in surrender to the lordship of Jesus Christ.
Nothing in my early life more clearly illuminated to me
exactly what that surrender means, and what it may cost,
than the following story about two twentieth century
young people who gave up their rights to themselves, took
up the cross, and followed.

John Stam was born early in the twentieth century in
Paterson, New Jersey. His father, Peter Stam, came from
Holland and established a building business but was known
in jails, hospitals, almshouses, and the poorest sections of
the city for his kind "servant heart." His six sons and three

daughters were brought up in a strong Christian home where Bibles were placed on the table three times daily and a chapter was read, each one taking a turn, before the food was served.

John was seated at his desk in business school one day in 1922 when he definitely handed over his life to the Lord. From that moment he knew he did not belong to himself but was forever to be at the service of his Master, Christ. His interest in making money waned. Things that lasted for eternity were all that mattered.

Elisabeth Alden Scott (directly descended from John and Priscilla Alden of the *Mayflower*) was born in the United States but brought up in China where her parents were missionaries. Her little sister described Betty, as she was always called, as tender and thoughtful. A lady who had had her as a student teacher when Betty was at Wilson College wrote to me:

"She impressed me the most, and is the only one I remember. She wore her hair then in braids, neatly around her head. She had about two white blouses that she wore with a dark skirt. Her manner was gentle, calm, with a quiet voice."

It was at Moody Bible Institute in Chicago that John Stam noticed in this girl something he had never found before, something that strangely attracted him. But his primary concerns were his studies and his weekend travels to preach in a church two hundred miles away. His feelings for this lovely woman were held so firmly in check that fellow students saw nothing.

Betty had assumed she would return to China as a missionary, but at Moody the continent of Africa came before her, especially the sufferings of lepers. Could she be willing to relinquish all that China meant and consecrate her life to service elsewhere? Her attention had been drawn also to the tall figure of John Stam, whose call to China was clear. The pull in that direction must have been powerful. "My Testimony" is the title she gives to lines that reveal not only her quite human and natural fear but also the gentle reassurance she received when she took that fear to her Lord.

> And shall I fear
> That there is anything that men hold dear
> Thou would'st deprive me of,
> And nothing give in place?
>
> That is not so—
> For I can see Thy face
> And hear Thee now:
>
> "My child, I died for thee.
> And if the gift of love and life
> You took from Me,
> Shall I one precious thing withhold—
> One beautiful and bright,
> One pure and precious thing withhold?
> My child, it cannot be."

Was it to be Africa or China? Marriage or singleness? The testings had to go deeper, as they must for all who set their faces as flint to follow the One who was crucified.

During her second year at Moody she sent another poem to her father. "This poem," she wrote, "expresses the distress of soul and fear of mind that were mine before I surrendered my all—even inmost motives, so far as I know—to God's control. The fourth stanza is His gracious acceptance of my unworthy self; the last tells of the joy, satisfaction, and peace of assured guidance that Christ my Savior gives me, now that He is Lord of my life."

Stand Still and See
I'm standing, Lord:
There is a mist that blinds my sight.

Steep, jagged rocks, front, left and right,
Lower, dim, gigantic, in the night.
  Where is the way?

I'm standing, Lord:
The black rock hems me in behind,
Above my head a moaning wind
Chills and oppresses heart and mind.
  I am afraid!

I'm standing, Lord:
The rock is hard beneath my feet;
I nearly slipped, Lord, on the sleet.
So weary, Lord! and where a seat?
  Still must I stand?

He answered me, and on His face
A look ineffable of grace,
Of perfect, understanding love,
Which all my murmuring did remove.

I'm standing, Lord:
Since Thou hast spoken, Lord, I see
Thou hast beset—these rocks are Thee!
And since Thy love encloses me,
  I stand and sing.

When the call to China had at last been confirmed, Betty Scott was among those who met weekly in the home of Dr. and Mrs. Isaac Page, who were with the China Inland Mission (founded by Hudson Taylor).

Also in the group was John Stam. Never had John preferred one girl above another. He had kept entirely free in heart and outward relations, expecting not only to go to China unmarried but to remain so for at least five years, since he hoped to engage in pioneering evangelistic work. He was ready to offer for the mountain tribes of the west or the Moslems of Sinkiang.

But now he faced a new challenge—that earnest and, to him, distracting member of the prayer group. The startling truth: He loved her. Now what?

We are not told what was said between them, only that, according to their biographer, "Betty, with her pure, sweet nature, did not hide from him that his love might be returned." She had found in this young man spiritual fellowship, a common missionary vision, a deep unity of heart in the things that mattered most.

The way, however, was not as clear as it might seem. Betty was to graduate a year before John. She had applied to the China Inland Mission and would sail in a few months. John had not yet been accepted by the C.I.M. He could not ask Betty to commit herself to an engagement when his way might not open to follow her to China. And what of the life of an itinerant evangelist? Was it compatible with marriage? Could he ask Betty to wait indefinitely?

Betty pressed forward with her plans, leaving the rest quietly in God's hands. She was to sail in the fall of 1931, and on her way west she had a day in Chicago. She and John had hours of talk and prayer down by the lake. It was Monday, so together they attended the C.I.M. prayer meeting at the Pages' that evening. They were to part, perhaps for a very long time. With no formal commitment such a parting was hard. But their watchword was "God first," and nothing was to supersede that loyalty.

John wrote to his father: "Betty knows that in all fairness and love to her, I cannot ask her to enter into an engagement with years to wait. But we can have a real understanding, keeping the interests of the Lord's work always first.

"The C.I.M. has appealed for men, single men, to itinerate in sections where it would be almost impossible to take a woman, until more settled work has been commenced. . . . Sometime ago I promised the Lord that, if fitted for this forward movement, I would gladly go into it, so now I cannot back down without sufficient reason, merely upon personal considerations. If, after we are out a year or two, we find that the Lord's work would be advanced by our marriage, we need not wait longer.

"From the way I have written, you and Mother might think that I was talking about a cartload of lumber, instead of something that has dug down very deep into our hearts. Betty and I have prayed much about this, and I am sure that, if our sacrifice is unnecessary, the Lord will not let us miss out on any of His blessings. Our hearts are set to do His will. . . . But this is true, isn't it, our wishes must not come first? The progress of the Lord's work is the chief consideration. So there are times when we just have to stop and think hard."

Eight months after Betty's sailing, John completed his studies, still uncertain about his acceptance by the C.I.M. He had yet to pass the physical and the requirements of the director and council. Chosen to deliver the class address at graduation, he spoke of responsibility for the spiritual needs of the world, of readiness to pay any price in obedience to God's call.

We must not retrench in any work which we are sure is in His will and for His glory. We dare not turn back because the way looks dark. . . . We may find ourselves at the place where we shall have to drink the bitter waters of Marah, but our Captain's presence can sweeten the most bitter. . . . The Lord of Hosts is present in every field of conflict, to encourage us and fight with us. . . . Who would not accept the challenge to go forward, "bearing precious seed"?

In July 1932, all barriers passed, John sailed, third class on the *Empress of Japan*, for China. He had written to Betty, asking the long-delayed question, hoping for her reply before sailing. It had not come. Doubts tormented him. He was so sure of his love for her—was she not sure of hers for him? Had he honestly desired nothing but the will of God? Was he willing to face life without this loved woman?

Betty had been designated to northern Anhwei but for various reasons had been delayed. Her parents were returning from furlough and asked her to meet them in Shanghai. While there she had to have a tonsillectomy, which kept her at the coast for several weeks. The timing of events was, as always, in God's hands. The *Empress of Japan* was rapidly nearing China, with John and his party on board.

The rest need hardly be told. What it meant to John to find that Betty was actually in Shanghai may be imagined. Their joy could not be contained. Nothing now prevented an engagement announcement, and everyone at headquarters seemed to share their happiness.

It was a long year that passed after John and Betty said good-bye in Shanghai. When they met again, it was the eve of their wedding.

"When the morning of October 25, 1933, dawned," Betty's mother wrote, "we were all filled with thankfulness that God had so wonderfully answered our prayers about the weather—a perfect day, not a cloud in the sky.

"The bride, on the arm of her father, wore a simple gown of white silk crepe. . . . On her lips was a sweet, happy smile, while she kept her eyes steadily on the face of the bridegroom. And he, waiting at the altar, had eyes for her alone."

The Stams' baby, Helen Priscilla, was born on September 11, 1934. In December John and Betty were captured by Chinese Communists, marched half-naked through the village streets, and beheaded. The baby was discovered thirty hours later by Mr. Lo, a pastor. She was lying on the bed, safe and warm in her zippered sleeping bag, apparently none the worse for her long fast. In the bag were an extra nightgown, some diapers, and two five-dollar bills, just enough to provide for the little rescue party, which included young mothers who fed the baby along the way.

Betty Scott Stam's prayer of irrevocable commitment and consecration, written many years earlier, acquired powerfully striking significance in view of the manner of their death.

> Lord, I give up all my own plans and purposes, all my own desires and hopes, and accept Thy will for my life. I give myself, my life, my all, utterly to Thee to be Thine forever. Fill me and seal me with Thy Holy Spirit. Use me as Thou wilt, send me where Thou wilt, work out Thy whole will in my life *at any cost,* now and forever.

Reflections on "At Any Cost"

- Think long and hard about Jesus' unequivocal demand for those who want to be His disciples. (See Luke 14:26–33.) Try to resist the temptation to list all the things you think these words *do not* or *cannot* possibly mean. List what they *do* mean—in your own life, today.
- Note John's self-discipline, holding firmly in check his attraction for Betty.
- Note Betty's willingness to go anywhere, even to Africa rather than China.
- Consider John's willingness to remain single for tribal work.
- Notice that John did not ask Betty for commitment as long as his acceptance by the mission was uncertain.
- Study the lessons of surrender, relinquishment, sacrifice, servanthood.

19

The Fear of Deprivation

He who did not spare his own Son, but gave him up for us all—how will he not also, along with him, graciously give us all things?

Romans 8:32

John and Betty Stam, long before they met, had individually made a lifetime decision to follow Christ. Remember her prayer: "I give myself, my life, my all, utterly to Thee to be Thine forever." Remember the moment at his desk when he handed over his life. Both were now the property of Someone Else.

Their loyalty to Christ was non-negotiable. With the psalmist, each could say, "My heart is steadfast; O God, my heart is steadfast" (Ps. 57:7). A steadfast heart is fixed, fastened, stable. Discovering their love for each other, they made no headlong rush for fulfillment but placed it wholly at God's disposal. He would always come first in their hearts. A steadfast heart is not prone to fickleness.

The lives of those who are not yet sure of their God are governed by fear, which is the antithesis of faith. The spectres of loneliness, rejection, deprivation, unfulfillment, the future, and, in the long run, of death, haunt such lives. "Perhaps God will not be nice to me. He has it in for me. I will always be miserable. If I try to trust God He will let me down. Better to trust a man or a woman, take the risk of fickleness—things *might*, after all, work out as I want them to."

George MacDonald's character, Sir Gibbie, finding that a flood was headed for the cottage, "was not terrified. One believing like him in the perfect Love and perfect Will of a Father of men, as the fact of facts, fears nothing. Fear is faithlessness. . . . A perfect faith would lift us absolutely above fear."

A man who has been rejected more than once begins to feel gun-shy. He fears that he is not marriageable material. Will he be consigned to lonely bachelorhood? If he tries again, will he be dumped? He has an overwhelming desire to be loved, to share his life with someone, to serve God with someone, to be a husband and father. Why won't God let someone into his life? he asks. When will it be his turn? He is afraid—afraid that the answer is NEVER. He feels deprived.

The fear of deprivation is "consuming my life," says one letter. The author sees marriage as a carrot on a stick that a sardonic God is dangling in her face. "I sit alone on a hill, separated from life as I would like it. Illusions visit and trick my heart and wound it time and time again. I get angry with God. I blame Him."

God never withholds from His child that which His love and wisdom call *good*. Recall the Lord's kind answer to Betty Scott's fear.

> "Shall I one precious thing withhold—
> One beautiful and bright,

One pure and precious thing withhold?
My child, it cannot be."

God's refusals are always merciful—"severe mercies" at times, as St. Augustine recognized (*Confessions* XI, 25), but mercies all the same.

I understand the fear so many describe. I know it well. But a long life has proved to me that most of the things I feared never happened. While it is perfectly true that some of my worst fears did, in fact, materialize, I see them now as "an abyss and mass of mercies," appointed and assigned by a loving and merciful Father who sees the end from the beginning. He asks us to trust Him.

Trust Him! Do what He says!

The more we learn to fear God the less we fear anything else. The fear of the Lord is the cure for boredom. It goes with living in the presence of God. It is a lamp in a dark place; it consumes malice and burns wrong thoughts. It is, according to Proverbs, *life*. It is the fruit of *humility*, and the first step to wisdom (Prov. 19:23; 22:4; 9:10).

Better a pittance with the fear of the LORD than great treasure and trouble in its train.

Proverbs 15:16 NEB

Fear God and obey his commands; there is no more to a man than this. For God brings everything we do to judgment, and every secret, whether good or bad.

Ecclesiastes 12:13 NEB

And then there's this promise: "He fulfills the desires of those who fear him" (Ps. 145:19). As we learn to fear, honor, and reverence Him, our desires themselves are gradually corrected. Things for which we once burned with desire lose their appeal. We learn, in the words of a prayer written in A.D. 492, to love what He commands and to desire nothing that He does not promise. Earth's "best bliss" will never fill our hearts, as Bernard of Clairvaux knew.

> Jesus, Thou joy of loving hearts,
> Thou fount of life, Thou light of men,
> From the best bliss that earth imparts,
> We turn unfilled to Thee again.

A thirty-something woman explains her willingness to endure multiple break-ups as springing from the notion of deprivation: "I have always seen myself as 'deprived,' I could never be a support to anyone else, so wrapped up in my own struggle. Today I read in 1 Peter 4:10 that we should employ our special gift in helping others as a good steward of the MANIFOLD grace of God. That word manifold hit me. It told me that God's grace is seen in all the different gifts He gives each of us, and we all share one another's. That does not sound like I am at all deprived. I even saw the most recent break-up as His GIFT to me.

"I realize my compromise was only the fruit of a wrong perspective of myself—deprived, instead of the richly blessed child of God that I am! I came from an alcoholic home. When I came to the Lord at nineteen I wanted to marry my boyfriend who had been with me for five years. I was so attached to him, but he wanted nothing to do with Jesus. I had to choose, and it was the HARDEST thing I ever did.

"Please pray for me that I will follow our Lord in His will on this matter and that I will trust His good plan for me and truly be enabled to leave my desire for marriage in God's hands.

"I appreciated so much hearing a reminder today that it is not always comfortable to do God's will. I am not comfortable right now, and I do tend to obey only when it doesn't hurt so much—until it hurts *too* much *not* to! I'm learning more and more to trust Him, no matter how things look, or how long they take to work out, not to judge who *God* is through the situation, but to judge the *situation* through who God is."

A strong lesson indeed, and one that God has to teach most of us repeatedly, so prone are we to grab what is "not quite" God's will. Our myopic vision easily concludes that God is depriving us of the one thing we believe would make us truly happy. A new temptation? Remember Eve! It was in her heart that the tyranny of self began, and all the rest of us fall prey to that same vicious tyranny. It is pride that lifts itself above God—*we* know better, we fear *He* is cheating us. *My* will is best. *His* will will be my downfall. Such forebodings come straight from the enemy, whose craft and power are great.

In today's social climate anyone who is not "in a relationship" is bound to feel inadequate, excluded, and deprived. If one is not giving rein to sexual desire, which is considered a basic need, he is likely to be told that he is denying his sexuality, which is denying *oneself*, which is denying one's identity. This is thought to be not only an infringement of each person's right to pursue a full and whole life but also pathological and therefore requiring professional counseling. May we keep in mind the promise of Scripture: "My God will meet all your needs" (Phil. 4:19). We are His children. We can trust our Father to be the best judge of just what our needs may be.

Dr. Diane Poythress, single, had the following dialogue with God in 1976.

"But God, I am not happy as I am."

"Would you be happy in any state? Would you not find reason to murmur against Me if you were married? What is happiness for you? Don't you think I am aware of your situation and concerned for you—I who gave My life blood for you in My only begotten Son?"

"You promised to supply all my needs. You said that they who seek the Lord will not lack anything good. So where is my mate?"

"In My sovereign wisdom, knowing your present measure of sanctification and the fulfilling life which I now have for you, singleness is My best and most precious gift. Do not use My promises against Me as though by loving Me you would be able to obtain your own ends."

"Why did you pass over me and not my friend?"

"I have other things for you, specially for you. She walks a different path with different problems which would only bring you much unhappiness. Do not envy, but rejoice and be glad for her."

"Will I be single forever?"

"You no more know that than you knew ahead of time the day of your conversion. These things are yet to be revealed and still remain in My secret will. Even marriage is not forever but only comes as My gift one day at a time. And now I will ask you some questions:

"To whom does tomorrow belong?"

"To You, God, I have given my life, plans, hopes, needs, my all. Therefore it is no longer mine to demand what I will. I do not even know whether You will deem it best that I have life tomorrow."

"Can tomorrow be different from the past?"

"No, Lord, Your grace all sufficient has been with me through some rough days, and if I can face tomorrow with Your grace as a single person then, yes, also the tomorrow forty years from now."

"Why do you want marriage?"

"Well, companionship and fulfillment of all my anxious needs. It won't provide that, will it? Only You can do that whether I'm married or single. Lord, help me to seek to be only what is most glorifying to You, that I may love You with the obedience of my life."

"I do not answer all the why's and wherefore's. I call you to trust in Me, in who I am, in My very nature. Believe me."

Here is the testimony of another who is learning to trust rather than to fear.

"By both Christian and worldly standards I was taught that if I wanted a guy I had to go get him. Not that I did anything drastic—I just called, and sometimes felt it was my duty to tell the guy how I felt. When I read your book I thought it was impossible to bring this part of my life under the type of control you wrote about. I thought, 'This woman needs to bring her 1940's mentality to the 1990s.' When I shared these thoughts with a friend she just laughed at me.

"Since then, in about a year's span, God has really changed my heart. First, I took a missions trip. It was a lesson in submission to God's will: First, I said I would not go. Then, I'd go if the man I was interested in went. Finally, I'd go if the Lord wanted me to. It was hard to get there, but I'm glad I did.

"Then, when I became interested in a man, I asked God for *His* permission first. When I tell people this, they don't understand. So I read P & P again. I no longer thought you needed to change your mentality. I saw you as a young woman going through the same struggles I was having. My friend laughed again.

"I then had to come to the point where I am now—waiting before the Lord about this man. I don't call. I don't go out of my way to talk to him—amazing for *me!* I'm working on being a woman for the Lord.

"I also realize it would not be the worst thing to go to heaven as a virgin!"

Another writes, "Being in submission to God far outdoes any joy given by my chasing my own whims."

And here's a man's testimony.

"The Lord taught me that preparing for marriage is 'not so much a matter of finding the right person as it is becoming the right person.' I began to concentrate on my relationship with Christ."

What could be better preparation for a Christ-centered marriage? "Husbands, love your wives, just as Christ loved the church and gave himself up for her to make her holy" (Eph. 5:25–26).

Reflections on "The Fear of Deprivation"

- Consider, before the face of God, your own fears. What do you intend to do with them?
- Can you share with others a fear that did materialize? Did that experience teach you something?
- Discuss judging who God is through a situation, as opposed to judging a situation through who God is.
- How does one *become* the right person?
- The Bible tells us what casts out fear. What is it? and for whom?

20

Guidance, Faith, Certainty

Trust in the LORD with all your heart
   and lean not on your own understanding;
in all your ways acknowledge him,
   and he will make your paths straight [direct your
   paths].

Proverbs 3:5–6

How shall I find the wisdom for the dreaded decision that must be made—tomorrow or next week or next year? How shall I find the strength to *do* what that decision will require?

These questions trouble many of us, and for none are they more intimidating than for those who seek guidance as to the right one to marry. How to differentiate between what God has wrought and what we ourselves have initiated?

"I finally woke up to the fact that this super-competent, infuriatingly logical, typical engineer had a heart of pure gold. For ten months I waited and prayed and edited my letters while God did His best to help me purify my imagination and hold loosely to my hopes and desires. I really had no concrete reason to think my feelings were reciprocated, so all I could offer God was a willingness not to pout if my hopes were unfulfilled." So goes a letter from one who says she just wants to *live faithfully.*

God surely hears that prayer when it is accompanied by obedience in the things that are perfectly clear. Both the wisdom and the strength will always be given, in perfect measure, when the time comes, if we take up quietly and faithfully the duties of today. Let us not make the mistake of directing our energies toward what is not today's business. The best preparation for the future is always the conscientious carrying out of what is given us today.

> Do not worry about what to say or how to say it. At that time you will be given what to say, for it will not be you speaking, but the Spirit of your Father speaking through you.
>
> Matthew 10:19–20

More than one man has asked me how Jim Elliot *knew* that he would not meet someone else that he liked better than me. "I wish I had that kind of confidence," one of them said, "but it looks idealistic, not realistic, to me."

I think Jim's answer would be quite simple: God had led him to this woman. The search was over. A man could spend the rest of his life (and many do) looking for someone better than the last one. This is where *faith* and *faithfulness* come in. Confidence in God. Has He promised to lead? Is He a faithful Shepherd? Will He make it impossibly difficult for His beloved sheep to discern His will, or will He keep His promise to direct your path?

"When does one say O.K., O.K.—*this* one?" they ask.

Maturity is the acceptance of limitations. Every choice made in life rules out a thousand other possibilities. Love, in the last analysis, is a choice. You marry her because you love her. Then, from the wedding day forward, you learn to love her because you married her. Circumstances do not change the obligation to fulfill the solemn vow.

I am sure that Jim did not make nearly so "big a deal" out of choosing a wife as men seem to today. Must they smell every rose in the world before discovering that the best one is in their own garden? A strong spiritual principle is to pray through things, think about them in the presence of God, and *stick with the decision.* Did God hear your prayer? Do you believe He wants you to do His will? Then "don't dig up in doubt what you planted in faith."

Believing prayer must be the practice of a Christian's whole life.

Rosalind Bell-Smith, born in London in 1864, was twelve years old when she heard a sermon on John 3:16 at a revival meeting. The love of God was presented with such fervor and intensity that she yielded herself absolutely to Christ and stood up, along with others, to confess Him publicly as her Lord and Master.

Her father having been an artist, she grew up with a great love for art and went to art school in Toronto. But there was a strong pull in two opposite directions: Should she give her life to painting or should she serve the Master to whom she belonged? In her mind the two were mutually exclusive.

When she was twenty she began to pray that if married life was what God wanted for her, He would give her a husband "wholly given up to Him and His service. I wanted no other."

One day in June 1885, she joined a group of art students bound for a picnic at Niagara Falls. On the same boat as they crossed the lake was another party, headed for a Bible conference. She envied the latter group—her heart was more with them than with her own crowd. On the return trip that evening both groups were on the boat again, plus others who had been at the Bible conference. The Bible teacher recognized Rosalind as the organist in the church where he had spoken the previous Sunday and invited her to join a mission group the following Saturday.

"We are to have a workers' meeting and tea, and I would like you to meet them all."

She was on the point of saying this was impossible when her brother whispered, "You have no time. You are going to England."

Partly to show her brother that she would do as she pleased ("and what a trifle can turn the course of a life!" she said later), she accepted the invitation on the spot.

As the teacher turned to leave, he called to a friend who looked to Rosalind like "a very shabby fellow." He was introduced as Jonathan Goforth, "our city missionary."

"I forgot the shabbiness of his clothes, however, for the wonderful challenge in his eyes!" she wrote.

"The following Saturday found me in the large, square workers' room of the Toronto Mission Union. Chairs were set all around the walls, but the center was empty. Just as the meeting was about to begin, Jonathan Goforth was called out. He had been sitting across the corner from me with several people between. As he rose, he placed his Bible on the chair.

"Then something happened which I could never explain, nor try to excuse. Suddenly I felt literally impelled to step across, past four or five people, take up the Bible and return to my seat. Rapidly I turned the leaves and found the Book worn almost to shreds in parts and marked from cover to cover. Closing the Book, I quickly returned it to the chair, and returning to my seat, I tried to look very innocent. It had all happened within a few moments, but as I sat there, I said to myself, 'That is the man I would like to marry!'

"That very day, I was chosen as one of a committee to open a new mission in the east end of Toronto, Jonathan

Goforth being also on the same committee. In the weeks that followed I had many opportunities to glimpse the greatness of the man which even a shabby exterior could not hide. So when, in that autumn he said, 'Will you join your life with mine for China?' my answer was yes, without a moment's hesitation.

"But a few days later when he said, 'Will you give me your promise that *always* you will allow me to *put my Lord and His work first,* even before you?' I gave an inward gasp before replying, 'Yes, I will, *always,'* for was not this the very kind of man I had prayed for? (Oh, kind Master, to hide from Thy servant what that promise would cost!)

"A few days after my promise was given, the first test in keeping it came. I had been (woman-like) indulging in dreams of the beautiful engagement ring that was soon to be mine. Then Jonathan came to me and said, 'You will not mind, will you, if I do not get an engagement ring?' He then went on to tell with the greatest enthusiasm of the distributing of books and pamphlets on China from his room in Knox [College]. Every cent was needed for this important work. As I listened and watched his glowing face, the visions I had indulged in of the beautiful engagement ring vanished. This was my first lesson in *real values.*"*

Dr. and Mrs. Goforth sailed for China in February 1888 and served there until 1935. He celebrated his seventy-sixth birthday on board ship, bound for Canada, where he died the following year.

* Rosalind Goforth, *Goforth of China* (Minneapolis: Bethany, n.d.), 47–49.

Reflections on "Guidance, Faith, Certainty"

- Does it make sense to pray for guidance about the future if we are not obeying in the thing that lies before us today? How many momentous events in Scripture depended on one person's seemingly small act of obedience! Rest assured: Do what God tells you to do now, and, depend upon it, you *will* be shown what to do next.

- Think about the statement, "What a trifle can turn the course of a life." God is in charge of all trifles. Nothing, with Him, is either great or small.

- What quality drew Rosalind to Jonathan?

- Note her acceptance of his desire to put God first. The first test of her sincerity came with the application of that principle. Does she dispute it? Change her mind?

- To accept the man is to accept his leadership, especially where sacrifice is asked.

21

The Discipline
of Waiting

Be still before the LORD and wait patiently for him;
do not fret.

Psalm 37:7

Is there a harder discipline than that of waiting, especially
when one's desires seem as wild and uncontrollable as a
prairie fire? A bitter young woman wrote, "I am sick of
waiting for God to get His act together. I feel hollow, empty,
empty, empty, and disappointed in Him."

Without real trust in who God is—trust in His never-
failing love and wisdom, we set ourselves up for disap-
pointment. Is He a good God? Will He give what is best?
If the answer is yes to both questions, it follows that He
will withhold many things that look attractive to us. It is
His mercy to withhold them. Shall we accuse Him of failure to get "His act" together or shall we echo the psalmist's

word, "I am still confident of this: I will see the goodness of the LORD in the land of the living. Wait for the LORD; be strong and take heart and wait for the LORD" (Ps. 27:13–14).

A man who chose to trust wrote, "It was a relief to realize that I didn't have to date my entire Christian campus and use the process of elimination to find the right wife! Not long after I had laid my desires on the altar, God brought into my life a wonderful lady. We are to be married in August, and expect to be jungle missionaries."

If we imagine that happiness is to be found by furious pursuit, we will end up in a rage at the unsatisfying results. If, on the other hand, we set ourselves to pursue the wise and loving and holy will of our Heavenly Father, we will find that happiness comes—quietly, in unexpected ways, and, surprisingly often, as the by-product of *sacrifice*.

Desire for marriage deeply tests our understanding of the cross. The cross of Christ means sacrifice. He gave Himself. He asks us who want to be disciples first to relinquish our rights to ourselves, then to take up the cross, and follow (Luke 9:23). The cross in Roman times was an instrument of torture. Jesus took it up gladly—in obedience to His Father and for love of you and me. If He asks us to take up our cross daily, He is asking us to be willing to suffer. What else can the cross mean?

Except for those far ahead of most of us in sanctity, waiting is a form of suffering—the difficulty of self-restraint, the anguish of unfulfilled longing, the bewilderment of unanswered prayer, my flesh and my heart failing, my soul breaking. These are indeed tribulations, and tribulation is the curriculum if we are to learn patience. We want answers *now*, right *now*, but we are required at times to walk in darkness.

Nevertheless, God is in the darkness.

"He knows the way that I take; when he has tested me, I will come forth as gold" (Job 23:10). I don't need to know the way. I need only to trust my Guide.

An engaged girl in Greece wrote, "For marriage we will have to wait until I finish university and my fiancé his doctorate, which will be in three years. We live in separate cities and he visits me every twenty days for just one or two days, and then goes back. We both find waiting a hard thing but we are learning that the grace of God is enough for each day and that waiting brings patience—and we need patience if we are to go through marriage. We have decided that where the will of God is, that is where we also want to be. Learning to rest in His hands and receive each day with thanksgiving is the lesson for now. Psalm 31:15, 'My times are in your hands,' is my comfort.

"I am learning some lessons in giving up my right to myself. It is helpful to know that others have been through the course and that they were made of clay as I am. The thought that I was bought with a price liberates me. Everything becomes simpler when the question comes to me, 'And what am I to do now? How do I react to this?' I *know* what I must do—the principle to which I always turn is this: I was bought at a price. I do not belong to myself. I don't have to listen to my emotional cries, my offended ego. I cannot do anything to keep my ego from bleeding, but I can ignore it and follow Christ."

This woman has expressed two supremely important lessons that the Austrian psychiatrist Victor Frankl learned in a radically different situation, concentration camp: that every freedom can be denied a man except the freedom to choose his attitude, and that suffering is not an obstacle to happiness but often the necessary means to it. To love a man and to be separated from him for a long period of time is hard. My Greek friend does not deny this but freely chooses the attitude of a child of God and in that choice finds joy.

"Sit still, my daughter," said Naomi to Ruth, "until thou know how the matter will fall" (Ruth 3:18 KJV).

Isaac Penington, a seventeenth-century author, wrote:

> What if the wicked nature, which is as a sea casting out mire and dirt, rage against thee? There is a river, a sweet, still, flowing river, the streams whereof will make glad thy heart. And learn but in quietness and stillness to retire to the Lord, and wait upon Him, in whom thou shalt feel peace and joy, in the midst of thy trouble from the cruel and vexatious spirit of this world.

Often a Christian man or woman falls prey to that cruel and vexatious spirit, wondering how to find marriage, who, when, where? It is on God that we should wait, as a waiter waits—not *for* but *on* the customer—alert, watchful, attentive, with no agenda of his own, ready to do whatever is wanted. "My soul, wait thou only upon God; for my expectation is from him" (Ps. 62:5 KJV). In Him alone lie our security, our confidence, our trust. A spirit of restlessness and resistance can never wait, but one who believes he is loved with an everlasting love, and knows that underneath are the everlasting arms, will find strength and peace.

God is in the waiting. "It is God who arms me with strength and makes my way perfect" (Ps. 18:32).

Reflections on "The Discipline of Waiting"

- Simplify your "agenda." Is it to be your "act" or God's?
- Would you agree that one of a man's problems in finding a wife is having too many choices? How did one man solve it?

- If our expectation is truly from Him, what is our response when He does the unexpected?
- Discuss happiness as a by-product of sacrifice. If you get bogged down in the discussion, Hebrews 12:2 may rescue you.
- Waiting: waste of time or necessary discipline?

22

Love Suffers Long

The fruit of the Spirit is love, . . . longsuffering. And they
that are Christ's have crucified the flesh with the affections
and lusts. If we live in the Spirit, let us also walk in the
Spirit.

Galatians 5:22, 24–25 KJV

Love always entails suffering. One who loves God is willing to wait.

My friend Frank Murray, born in the early part of the
twentieth century, is a man of godly strength, kindness,
tenderness, and delightful humor. He waited a very long
time for Lois.

When he was ten years old the missionary community
in Maine where he had grown up was disbanded. His wid-
owed mother moved her five children to Auburn, Maine,
where life in the "wide world" was new and amazing to
the highly impressionable boy. Not the least of the shocks
concerned the breezy attitude toward love and marriage
that permeated society in 1920. Attitudes, which by today's

standards would be considered Puritan, were horrifying to him. With his mother's vigilant help he closed his eyes and ears (most of the time) to all the talk and the stories and the hideous immoral suggestions he heard on the school playground and in the alley where he picked up the newspapers he was to deliver.

"At the age of puberty," he writes, "the problems began to multiply, but I am thankful to be able to say that my brother and I turned away from temptation, and graduated from high school with a generally unblemished record. But not without attacks on our hearts, both of us. Human nature being what it is, and flirtations or worse all around us, we had to 'flee youthful lusts' like everyone else who values a clean conscience.

"In college I was surrounded with female attractions, but somehow the good Lord had sealed off my heart so effectively that no one appealed to me, except perhaps for an hour. I knew that by the standards I had been brought up there was no one that I could even contemplate as a wife in all that academic framework, so I shut and locked my heart's door."

In the summer of 1932 he met Frank Sandford, who, he writes, was "the greatest and kindest man I had ever known—his face shone, his voice entranced me, his kindness was without parallel, and most of all his reflection of Jesus Christ was perfectly amazing. I loved him from the first moment, and also feared him in a way, because I felt dirty and unworthy in his presence. It seemed to me that when he found out what I was really like he would send me home. Nevertheless for some reason I was allowed to stay on, and I found that my poverty of spirit was the unexpected ticket to great blessing."

It was through Mr. Sandford that Frank Murray was introduced to Jesus as a real Savior. This was the most crucial event in his life. This kindled a deep desire to see other students know that Savior. Taking part in a campaign of

prayer for the colleges of Maine he enlisted the coopera-
tion of, among others, one young lady from Ottawa, Kansas,
named Lois Abram, whom he hardly knew. Protesting her
lack of special talent, wondering what good she could possibly do, she nevertheless agreed to pray.

When he went to a Christian convention in Boston at
Christmastime, 1933, Frank met in the front hall a tall,
slender, dark-eyed young woman whom he thought he
had never met. She introduced herself as Lois Abram.

"We shook hands, and something happened to me right
then," Frank writes.

"I should explain that my three sisters and my mother
were of a rather hearty physical make-up, with firm solid
handshakes, and I was unprepared for this slim, delicate
hand that was practically lost in mine. I tried to forget it
and even to feel amused at such a frail substitute for practical usefulness in hands. But the memory of that feeling
persisted, even though she told me later she had no thought
whatever of conveying anything beyond mere courtesy."

Lois, "this frail, pale, undernourished-looking woman,"
who had driven her Model A Ford all the way from Kansas,
sat opposite Frank at the large supper table. "And where
I had had only a dim view of her in the poorly lighted hall-
way I now saw that she had lovely dark brown eyes and
a hauntingly attractive face, besides the fact that her clothes
were in rare good taste. I was smitten."

There was no opportunity for an acquaintance to develop
at that conference. Frank believed it was the mercy of God
that he did not actually fall in love then. In fact, in the
whirl of college life (in addition to the usual pressures of
studies, he was editing a monthly publication and was
preparing for a cross-Canada debating trip) he very nearly
forgot Lois altogether. He graduated in June 1934, weary
in body and soul. Marriage was the last thing on his mind.
Finding a job, no small matter during the Depression, was
first.

He had two job offers, but his friend Mr. Sandford challenged him to spend the summer in prayer about his future life work. The thought of losing two teaching opportunities made the decision an agonizing one, but he took the advice, which changed the course of his life. He began evangelization and Bible studies for college men in New Hampshire and Maine, then headed west on a missionary journey with his sister and three other men. Mr. Sandford issued one stern injunction: there were to be "no romantic sidelines." "We were to attend strictly to the Lord's business and not muddy it up with love affairs, public or private. He made sure that we all understood this, for he knew from long experience that nothing confuses soul-winning more quickly than attempts at romantic conquest. So that was settled."

Mr. Sandford had directed the team to a widow in Kansas who was glad to open her home to gospel workers. They were warmly received by her—and by her daughter, none other than Lois Abram.

"I discovered a radiant person there that I could scarcely connect with the disconsolate woman who had left Boston two years before. Firmly determined to carry out orders I took charge of myself and avoided any personal exchanges that were not completely general and necessary. In fact, I told myself she was 'not my type' anyway. (How little we know in advance what our 'type' is!) Still, I could not seem to forget the lovely white hat and beautiful red and white dress that she was wearing when we first arrived. Such good taste!

"These thoughts and a few others like them I confided to no one—I mean *no one*. I didn't even meditate on them myself when alone. But I did notice Lois's complete unselfishness and the way she poured out her soul in our prayer meetings. Even if we had been disposed to treat the whole expedition as a sort of lark, her complete seriousness would have been a rebuke. I thought to myself that here was an undiscovered asset to the Kingdom. Her common sense and devotion combined were a complete denial of her own self-estimate of worthlessness."

When the time came to leave, the fact hit Frank that he did not want to. His sister embraced Lois with a few tears. Lois then "turned to me with shining eyes and gripped my hand as though she did not want to let go. Or was it I who gripped her hand?

"My heart gave a great heave, but I tried to hide it with casual conversation. We chugged away, left Kansas behind.

"I could not forget. I was twenty-five years old, my brother was engaged. Was I ordained to a life of celibacy? Did God have no wife in mind for me? I don't remember feeling dissatisfied, much less rebellious, but still that lovely person back in Kansas would not be banished from my mind. What was she doing? Was she getting attached to someone else?"

He decided to write a letter, confiding his feelings to his spiritual father, Mr. Sandford, who knew the Abrams well, and whose judgment he completely trusted. There followed eight weeks of Bible study during which he wondered if his letter had been read. Called at last to Mr. Sandford's room he was questioned about Lois. Yes, Mr. Sandford knew her very well, esteemed her highly, but she was frail—did Frank know how frail? Could she "bang around" on college journeys? Perhaps there was a more buoyant, healthy woman somewhere who would be better able to stand by him. Furthermore, Frank was "only" twenty-five. Why the hurry?

"Somehow I accepted his words fully and did not fret even for a day. God's Spirit came to my aid and did not let me moon around and pity myself."

Sometime later Lois cast in her lot with the College Company, as they called the little mission group, full time. There was no shadow of intimacy or even mutual understanding between her and Frank, though both, he felt sure, enjoyed the propinquity.

"This state of affairs went on without any new development for nearly five years. Yet there was a providence that heightened our proximity." Working together each month on the printing of a small paper the two sat side by side for hours at a time, only about two feet apart, setting up type. "Such feelings as at times swirled through my breast! Yet, as far as I could see there was nothing—absolutely nothing—in her looks or acts that could be called responsive. She later told me that she was of the same opinion about me. She couldn't see the slightest sign of encouragement in my tone or manner. . . .

"If I do say it, it was a triumph of grace over nature, and only bore witness to the pure ministry of the man of God we both trusted. Without his restraining spirit I would never have been able to exercise such self-control, nor she either, I expect."

Sometime in 1939 Lois told Mr. Sandford, simply and in a few words, how she felt about Frank. He treated the subject seriously, recognizing the reality of this woman's commitment to Christ and the utter absence in her of any catering to her own desires. Much later she explained to Frank that she had been driven nearly to distraction by fears that his affections might be turning elsewhere, and if so she wanted to know and not harbor false hopes.

Mr. Sandford then went to Frank and asked him if he was still interested in Lois. Not a word was said, of course, of her talk with him. Frank's answer was a strong affirmative, and he was told to go ahead and do as he felt led. *"Did I ever feel led!"*

It was time for Frank to make his monthly trip to the printshop. Not seeing any opportunity to talk with Lois alone he wrote her a note expressing his heart's desire and asking what she felt.

"The fact must be kept in mind that so far I had had no overt encouragement whatever. For all I knew this quiet, self-contained woman might be secretly pledged to some other man. We had never talked together alone, had never corresponded except on college affairs, and had evinced no slightest outward signs of interest in each other. Such a procedure would have been easy with my sister Jean as intermediary, but it would have been contrary to all our training.

"Let me emphasize here that I regard our approach to courtship as standard for Christians. There is so much illicit love nowadays, and so much flirting and boisterous joking about even licit love, that the sacredness of it all seems to get worn away before young people are hardly into their teens. The long tension between Lois and me was not a bad thing; it settled us down into serious counting of the cost and winnowed out every trace of carnal sentiment that could have sullied the whole experience.

"So I placed that note where she would be sure to see it on a Friday night and got no answer until Saturday night. All day long I was tormented with the thought that she might reject my proposal, but when we met in the typesetting room that evening she passed me another note, as brief as mine, that said in effect: 'Yes.' That was that but even then we did not feel free to publish our understanding until we had both reported to our spiritual overseer. We wished to have him do the announcing. But joy flowed like a river just the same, and we managed a long series of further notes."

Weeks went by before Mr. Sandford suggested that Frank use the quiet of the next morning to go for a walk with Lois. He would make the announcement later on in the day ("a glorious suggestion!" thought Frank). Not one person in that close fellowship knew what was going on except the three.

About nine o'clock on that lovely August morning the two walked side by side, though not yet hand in hand, to the spot Frank had selected, a maple grove on a hill.

"She was trembling and so was I. It seemed like a dream that might end at any moment. We had waited so long; and now could it really be possible that this our joy was being made full? We found a place to sit side by side. I looked at her and she looked at me, for the first time not furtively but at length.

"As a matter of fact, I did not know what to do. I had not touched her, and didn't feel free to, she was so pure and sacred. Yet we both knew that this was the beginning of a new chapter that would last perhaps forever. So I fell back on the Scripture. I opened my Bible to Isaiah 62, that wonderful chapter about the City of Zion and the Land of Beulah, married to Israel and to Israel's God. I read it through to her, though she knew it as well as I, and told her that I believed our marriage was going to be of that quality.

"Looking back on it now, I fear I was somewhat pretentious, but at the time was deadly serious; and it may be that God honored my use of this golden chapter to dignify our marriage. Anyway, I prayed before daring to touch her (and perhaps she prayed too; I can't remember). Then we embraced, rather awkwardly, in fact. But love was sealed then and there in August of 1940, and that was the beginning of a Psalm of Life that lasted for forty-eight years."

Reflections on "Love Suffers Long"

The following facts in the Murray story are well worth studying:

- A man's heart was "sealed."
- He submitted to spiritual authority.

- His lips were sealed on the subject of Lois.
- He did not allow his thoughts to dwell on her.
- He was attracted by her unselfishness, her prayer life, her radiance, her quietness.
- He confided in a third party, his spiritual mentor.
- He allowed no self-pity.
- The two had had time to count the cost and winnow out carnal sentiment.
- Men take note: Lois had offered *no* overt encouragement whatever. The first move had to be Frank's.

23

Is Chastity Possible?

We instructed you how to live in order to please God, as in fact you are living. Now we ask you and urge you in the Lord Jesus to do this more and more. For you know what instructions we gave you by the authority of the Lord Jesus.

It is God's will that you should be sanctified: that you should avoid sexual immorality; that each of you should learn to control his own body in a way that is holy and honorable, not in passionate lust like the heathen, who do not know God.

1 Thessalonians 4:1–5

Is chastity possible?

Yes.

It is always possible to do the will of God.

Sex is *not* an irresistible force. Hormones are not autonomous.

Following a talk on chastity a strapping athlete approached me and said, "Holy cow, lady—ya *gotta* have *sex!*"

"Really?" said I. "Where did you get that idea? Hundreds of thousands have lived entirely without it."

Person and *self* are the words that define the moral universe of the majority today. When a famous basketball player makes no bones about the fact that his being HIV positive is the result of relations with countless women, and another tells the world he's had sex with twenty thousand, hardly anyone blinks. But when an athlete named A. C. Greene succeeds in remaining celibate even during the nine years he's been playing basketball, resisting the advances of hordes of attractive groupies, he makes the front page of a Sunday magazine. He is even allowed to speak to high school assemblies about abstinence. That makes a lot of people blink.

One columnist said that a woman who chooses not to fall into bed with a man finds herself branded with the scarlet letter *A*, which now stands for *abstinence*.

The hallowed virtue now is self-love. Where we used to take it for granted that we ought to learn unselfishness, we have been bombarded for several decades with the ideology of the self. Self-fulfillment, self-realization, self-esteem, self-awareness, self-actualization have been endlessly propagated in schools, universities, the media, and from many a pulpit both liberal and conservative. It is one of the signs of the "terrible times in the last days," according to 2 Timothy 3:2. "People will be lovers of themselves," without love, without self-control.

Ironically, as I write, I find some secular thinkers are coming to their senses and beginning to criticize this obsession, while the self-help section in many Christian bookstores still takes up several aisles. The ancient concepts of self-control, self-denial, self-abandonment, and self-sacrifice find little place there. And one's simple *duty?* What is that? A word without content in the minds of millions.

Libido does not cancel the possibility of choice.

To choose chastity has always been possible. It is possible today, as one couple proved.

"Principles once so cloudy have become clear. Two statements stay with me: (1) 'The heart set to do the Father's will need never fear defeat' and (2) 'If virginity is to be preserved, lines must be drawn. Why put yourself in any situation where the lines become smudged and obscure? Why take the risks?'

"I am so filled with joy when I think of the beauty of sex within marriage. I am so glad that I waited!

"In 1990 Jerry and I ran into each other at a seminar where [the speaker] talked about being content in Christ as a single. Both of us committed at that time to rest in the Lord and wait patiently for Him. We were content being single. It is awesome how Christ gives a peace that passes all understanding!

"Well, one week after the seminar Jerry asked me out. We had a nice dinner and even talked about the seminar. It was incredible to me to meet a man totally committed to Christ, who had maintained a life of purity for almost twenty-nine years, and had godly standards like my own. On November 30, 1991, he told me for the *first* time that he loved me and wanted to back that up with a life-long commitment. We were married six months later on May 23, 1992. It was the happiest day of my life! We have an excellent marriage and I credit that to several factors:

1. The Lord Jesus Christ, who saved us and made us new creatures;
2. godly parents who instructed us;
3. godly teachers who taught us God's Word; and
4. a firm foundation that was laid in our dating relationship.

"We started out as friends and built the relationship. Through time, a true love developed. The physical part of our relationship came last. We did not talk about our marriage or our love until he had proposed. I am so glad we did it God's way!"

Chastity is rare, but it is always possible. "The one who is in you is greater than the one who is in the world" (1 John 4:4).

The "traditional" view has been handed down to us by no less an authority than God Himself, yet it is deeply disturbing to find that abstinence, chastity, virginity, sexual purity are seldom if ever the subjects of sermons in most churches today. It is often taken for granted that as free moral agents, we may choose whatever feels good or seems "right for us." Sex is considered a basic need and becomes therefore a *right* that no one ought to be denied.

But God's word is plain. "God did not call us to be impure, but to live a holy life" (1 Thess. 4:7).

A holy life is a *whole* life. The words *whole* and *holy* derive from the same root. The word used for passionate lust covers a wide range of sexual interaction.

The very struggle in which we find ourselves when sexual longings are unfulfilled is *God's call:* Come to me. I will give you rest. But we must take *His* yoke—a burden indeed, but a light one, He promises. It is much lighter than the yoke our self-will imposes.

Corinth in Paul's day was a city full of corruption, blatant sexual sin, and pornographic obsession. He warned the Christians there not to associate with anyone who called himself a (Christian) brother who was sexually immoral. He did not forbid association with non-Christians, regardless of their sins, for it was no business of his to judge those outside the church. It was important, however, to remember that there were Christians in the church who had been fornicators, idolaters, adulterers, male prostitutes, homosexual offenders, thieves, greedy, drunkards, slanderers, and swindlers.

> But you were washed, you were sanctified, you were justified in the name of the Lord Jesus Christ and by the Spirit of our God. . . .

The body is not meant for sexual immorality, but for the Lord. . . . Do you not know that your bodies are members of Christ himself? Shall I then take the members of Christ and unite them with a prostitute? Never! Do you not know that he who unites himself with a prostitute is one with her in body? . . .

Flee from sexual immorality. All other sins a man commits are outside his body, but he who sins sexually sins against his own body. Do you not know that your body is a temple of the Holy Spirit who is in you, whom you have received from God? You are not your own; you were bought with a price. Therefore honor God with your body.

1 Corinthians 6:9–20

C. S. Lewis gives three reasons why it is especially difficult for us to desire—let alone to achieve—complete chastity.

In the first place our warped natures, the devils who tempt us, and all the contemporary propaganda for lust, combine to make us feel that the desires we are resisting are so "natural," so "healthy," and so reasonable, that it is almost perverse and abnormal to resist them. . . .

In the second place, many people are deterred from seriously attempting Christian chastity because they think (before trying) that it is impossible. But when a thing has to be attempted, one must never think about possibility or impossibility. . . .

Thirdly, people often misunderstand what psychology teaches about "repressions." It teaches us that "repressed" sex is dangerous. But "repressed" is here a technical term: it does not mean "suppressed" in the sense of "denied" or "resisted."

Mere Christianity, chapter 5 of the section
on Christian behavior

Here is the battleground, and none more crucial, in the lives of young people who determine to be holy. There is an "Ancient Foe who seeks to work [them] woe. His craft and power are great, and armed with cruel hate, on earth is not his equal" (Martin Luther's hymn "A Mighty Fortress"). Until Jesus Christ is Lord of the sex life He is not Lord of one's *life*. Not only is every act meant to be subject to His holy will, but every thought must be brought into captivity to Christ. And this "captivity" turns out to be not bondage, not repression, not misery, but JOY!

A sophomore at Indiana University described in a letter to me some of God's working in her life.

"God has been *so faithful* in working with my heart and will, so patient in gently, continually opening His arms, always saying, 'COME.' He is so loving! . . . The thought struck me that you must see and hear of a lot of depressing things in American youth and concerning our culture these days. I wish I could let you know that God is still really at work in my life, in my family's life, and in many of my friends' lives as well.

"This stanza [of a poem by Amy Carmichael] has been my heart's cry lately.

> I wish Thy way.
>> But when in me myself would rise
>> And long for something otherwise,
> Then, Holy One, take sword and spear
>> And slay.

"Now seems to be a time of security in simply *not knowing* the future. I have no boyfriend, and must say it's been a struggle at times, since I see many others happy with theirs (my sister, for example—he is so godly and wonderful, I must say!). I'm also a little 'odd' by 'normal' standards in this area, because God has given me the conviction that I am not to kiss before marriage. I struggled last year while dating a neat guy—and came out knowing that this no kissing rule was God's will for me, no matter what others think. My parents wholeheartedly support this, and even the younger children are intrigued and respectful—and, so far, imitative. Thank You, Lord!

"So I am truly grateful that God has kept me physically pure by sparing me from giving away a part of my heart in kissing. I do want *His way.* It takes faith when doubts flood in, such as, 'Will I ever marry?' and 'I feel worthless!' God is teaching me to chew on the TRUTH of His Word and to immediately humble myself in coming before Him for protection and help. The verse He gave me today is Psalm 119:165, 'Great peace have they who love your law, and nothing can make them stumble.'"

Reflections on "Is Chastity Possible?"

- To commit oneself to chastity in today's world is to accept opprobrium. One will probably be thought very odd and perhaps abnormal. Can you stand the rude questions?
- The self movement encourages many kinds of self-indulgence. How has it affected you?
- Our struggles are God's call: Come to Me.
- Note Lewis's three reasons why it is difficult even to desire chastity. What does he say about impossibilities?
- Commitment to chastity requires faith and patience. It also requires a clear *decision* as to where you will draw the line. "Never pull down a fence till you know why it was put up."
- Memorize Isaiah 50:7: "Because the Sovereign LORD helps me, I will not be disgraced. Therefore have I set my face like flint, and I know I will not be put to shame."
- Given the great obstacles to chastity, is it worth the effort?

24

Sowing in Tears

Those who sow in tears
will reap with songs of joy.

Psalm 126:5

Only once do we read of Jesus weeping. It was when He was with Mary and Martha, whose brother Lazarus had died. His agony in the Garden of Gethsemane brought forth sweat like great drops of blood. None of us will ever know that measure of agony, when "desperate tides of the whole great world's anguish" crashed over the Son of Man. But we know what tears are about. The surrender of the heart's deepest longing is perhaps as close as we come to an understanding of the cross. This trial of our faith is *crucial*, a word that derives from the Latin *crux*, cross. Our own experience of crucifixion, though immeasurably lesser than our Savior's, nonetheless furnishes us with a chance to begin to know Him in the fellowship of His suffering. In every form of our own sufferings, He calls us to that fellowship. Ought we not to be thankful, then, for that?

"Did you really wrestle with God?" a girl wrote to me. "I mean, roll-around-on-the-ground wrestle over these issues? I desperately desire the Lord to lead a man of godly character to pursue me, rather than vice versa. My trial is what to do about how I *feel*. I have prayed and prayed for an answer about him. Even after a day of fasting the only answer I got was *keep waiting*."

Yes. I know. I wrestled. With a pang I still recall that early morning in Ecuador in 1952—it was not yet light— when Jim Elliot left Quito for the eastern jungle. In love for more than four years, we were still not engaged. We were not committed to anything except the will of God. We had no answer but *keep waiting*. Would I see him again? Would we ever marry? I cried so bitterly my landlady heard me and rushed to my room.

Janet Erskine Stuart wrote:

> It is good that we should have to submit to what we do not understand. It teaches us the laws of faith and hope.
> It is good that we should have to do what we should rather not, in circumstances not of our choice.
> It is good that there should be always something to prick us on, something to remind us that we are in an enemy's country, belong to a marching column.
> It is good that we should meet with checks and failures in what we undertake, to keep us humble and prayerful.
> All these things belong to sowing in tears.
> God seems to have laid out the order of things in His Church, not for a general and brilliant triumph but for the hidden sanctification of the individual souls which compose it.
>
> *Prayer in Faith*

A man describes the girl he loves and then asks, "Can I be trusting God and still aching to be with that wonderful girl?"

Of course. When we have committed desire to Christ the desire does not necessarily fade, but it no longer dominates. Commitment is a deliberate conveying to another the control of that desire. We have seen this in the stories of Tom Griffith, Fred Malir, Dick Hillis, Hudson Taylor, Frank Murray, and others.

"Is it possible to trust God so much I won't be lonely?"

Probably not, at least for most of us, because we need the lessons loneliness brings. It is *good* for us, for that hidden sanctification.

"What about all this impatience I feel, that I don't want?"

The answer is the same. Wrestling, loneliness, impatience—for our hidden sanctification. The trial of our faith is a thing more precious than gold. Must we go for the gold? We must.

The longing for human love is powerful, but there is a more powerful one. It is for God, although few identify it correctly until they have tried many other springs.

> My people have committed two sins:
> They have forsaken me,
>   the spring of living water,
> and have dug their own cisterns,
>   broken cisterns that cannot hold water.
>
> Jeremiah 2:13

The woman at the well knew that emptiness. She met the One who alone could fill her heart. God wants to fill ours and He is wonderfully patient as we struggle to offer up heart, will, mind, intelligence, passion, emotions, affections. Although painful, it is only one day at a time, and we have the promised help of a Heavenly Father who is more compassionate than any earthly father.

It has taken me a long time to realize that it is these very struggles that God *provides*. Yes, I say provides. He does not let them "just happen." In St. Paul's chapter about his own troubles (hard-pressed, perplexed, persecuted, struck down), he says, "All this is for your benefit, so that the grace that is reaching more and more people may cause thanksgiving to overflow to the glory of God" (2 Cor. 4:15). They are good for us and good for those who watch us.

A prospective missionary, in love with a man who also plans to be a missionary, tells me she has been learning what a Christ-centered relationship really is. She feels lonely at times, "yet I am learning to praise God. He has given me so much 'life and more abundantly.' I would not trade the joy, the learning, and the experiences I have now for anything. Knowing that I am in His will is contentment that is far beyond what 'doing my own thing' could ever bring."

Because we are sinners and live in a fractured world, we must have tribulation. Jesus promised it—but (don't forget) He added, "Cheer up! I have overcome the world!"

Therefore it is as we realistically name and accept the truth about ourselves that we come to see that He alone is the Living Fountain. He alone can save us from ourselves.

A friend who often writes to me reveals what the surrender of her longings costs.

"It should be no surprise that He wants *everything* in us. We are all His doing, nothing comes into being, has breath, has anything, without HIM, so it follows that our little deaths and tremendous joys should begin and end with HIM. Thus, the origin of our daily wars.

"My little wars come and go. Exceedingly anxious about my lovelife, I fight on the front lines of desire and longings. . . . I pull myself away, with head lowered and heart aching for the power to believe—that in giving up all of these games, I will not lose a step (as HE withholds no good thing).

"I still hear the enemy's shouts, trying to convince me that my retreat is in vain, yet I have chosen somehow (God only knows that at times it's like bridling a bucking bronco!) to keep silent in my world of feelings and dreams, wishes and desires, and to lay them down at the altar of God, walking away believing there are, indeed, higher stakes in all of this than mere desires.

"We both know that seeking to save one's own life is the very thing Jesus warned us not to do. Christ has never told us to seek what we want, He has told us to seek only Himself! I'm finding that this war will rage, I suspect, until my dying day, but I hold onto the hope that it brings me nearer, dearer, closer to Him."

There's the testimony of one person who desperately *wants* marriage but even more desperately *wills* the will of God, whether or not that includes marriage. This is evidence of grace in that life. No one of us could manage without God's marvelous, infinite, matchless grace. It is the pouring out of the gift of Himself to the heart that *wills* to receive Him, the heart that is open.

An unknown friend in Eastern Europe writes, "I am a Christian only since the summer of 1987 when I first met the living God who is my Lord now. It was the first time I had to face the problem of obedience. So I want a real, living God who has the power of making me free from the old life but who at the same time wants to realize His own will in the new one. And after a long struggle I decided to take Him up on His offer and say yes. Of course, He was faithful and had given me really a new mind, a new heart, a new life. Ever since then I regard obedience as one of the most important things in walking with God. Maybe that is why I feel your books so near to me. To be obedient is difficult and I found that commitment has to be renewed again and again.

"When I read the life story of Jim Elliot, *Shadow of the Almighty,* I understood that I have to be faithful in *every-*

thing I do. I think you can guess what happened. I fell in love."

She tells of meeting a man who "sticks to the Word of God and is not one to compromise in what he understands as God's will." He was kind but showed no sign of any affection.

"I could not be anything in his eyes but a mere chit. But I would like to have a husband like him. I know it is pretty hopeless. What can I offer him, what can I give him? I asked myself. All this seemed so girlish and I kept it a secret.

"I asked God if He would give me this man as a husband. His answer: 'The Lord takes pleasure in those who fear Him, who trust in His love' (Psalm 147:11). I understood that there was no definite answer because God wants me to trust Him even if I do not know or understand the way He is leading me. Jesus is the Good Shepherd. I simply have to believe that He knows what He is doing, where He is leading me and I have to follow."

God gave the girl work to do that made it impossible for her to see this man without neglecting the work.

"God's intention was clear. No green light, all roads blocked. Since then, although occasionally I did have a good excuse for going where I might have seen him, I stayed. For seven months now I have not seen him. Sometimes I feel I cannot endure it any more and I will just get on a bus and go, but God's word is coming silently and convinces me that it is better for me not to. I know He is right. If I met him it would be even harder to stand still, wait, do the work God has given. The Lord has kept me this far, but even if I can stop my feet from walking to him, I cannot stop thinking and dreaming. . . . This fight seems so hopeless. I cannot even gather the strength to *want* what God wants. It is like the state Paul describes in Romans 7. With my mind I know that Jesus Christ can save me from this situation, but how? How can I offer it up without taking it back again? I do not know what else to do. Please give me advice!"

My advice: Do the next thing. Lift up your heart. Trust that God took seriously your offering and rest in the knowledge that nothing *but* trust is required of you at this moment.

Reflections on "Sowing in Tears"

- Examine your willingness, in the light of your life's goal, to sow in tears.

- Do you agree that *God* provides the situations that cause us to struggle? Would you state it differently? (See Romans 8:28–29; Psalm 119:91; Psalm 16:5; Proverbs 16:33.)

- Have our human sufferings in this fallen world anything to do with Christ's sufferings? (See Philippians 1:29 and Colossians 1:24.)

- Can you see love's longing as a portion of the fellowship of His suffering?

- "Love is an absolute point of departure." True or false?

- Note will versus desire—my friend in Europe did *not* get on the bus. She willed against herself and for God. Although her emotions remained active and alive, they were no longer at her disposal. They had been given to God.

- One cannot always control feelings, but one can choose not to walk into temptation.

25

Temptation

Blessed is the man that endureth temptation: for when he is tried, he shall receive the crown of life, which the Lord hath promised to them that love him.

James 1:12 KJV

It is no good praying, "Lead us not into temptation" and then deliberately walking straight into it. Young people tell me of parking the car or going to his or her dorm room or apartment, with no intention of "doing anything," and then, somehow or other, "things happen." Surprised?

One who is in good earnest about maintaining purity will avoid, at all cost, dangerous people, parties, and places. It is not very difficult to absent ourselves physically. It's easy enough not to open the bedroom door, but to close the door of the mind is something else.

The battleground is the mind. To pray, "Deliver us from evil" lays on us the responsibility to struggle against the evil in our minds, for that is where trouble begins and where it must be conquered. God expects us to do our part.

The will He has given us He will not invade, for it is inherent in the nature He designed that our wills must be free. We *can* choose—to yield or not to yield, to go to the party or not to go, to be seduced or to flee. We can make up our *minds*.

> Though we live in the world, we do not wage war as the world does. The weapons we fight with are not the weapons of the world. On the contrary, they have divine power to demolish strongholds. We demolish arguments and every pretension that sets itself up against the knowledge of God, and we take captive every thought to make it obedient to Christ.
>
> 2 Corinthians 10:3–5

God has given us the spirit of power and of love and of a sound mind (see 2 Tim. 1:7 KJV). We can close that mind to sinful suggestions. Amy Carmichael says:

> We can lose this power through disuse, or increase it by use, by the daily discipline of the inner man in things which seem small and by reliance upon the word of the Spirit of Truth. . . . Do not fight the thing in detail: turn from it. Look ONLY at your Lord. Sing. Read. Work.
>
> *Gold by Moonlight* (Christian Literature Crusade)

"When the enemy comes in like a flood, the Spirit of the Lord will put him to flight" (Isa. 59:19, footnote).

Who of us does not feel our weakness, fear being overcome by temptation too strong for us? All the more reason to keep out of the way of it. Jesus told the disciples to *watch* and *pray* in order not to enter into temptation. This is what watching means. Be on the alert. Be honest about your weakness. Stay clear of the thing that tempts you. *Flee!* When Potiphar's wife tried to seduce her husband's faithful servant Joseph, he didn't hang around. He ran for his life. Paul told Timothy to *flee* youthful lusts. Get out of there—NOW!

"Turn your back on the turbulent desires of youth and give your positive attention to goodness, faith, love and peace in company with all those who approach God in sincerity" (2 Tim. 2:22 *Phillips*).

Ulysses was extremely tough on himself. He made no boast that he could "handle" the song of the Sirens. He needed protection and had himself tied up and his ears plugged with wax. We need to harness ourselves firmly, renounce sometimes even legitimate things in order not to be taken in by the evil that lurks at every turn. We can't be too careful. Much better to be too strict than too easy. Strictness is the safer side.

"And miss out on all the fun?" Some of it, perhaps—and then discover the *joy* of self-discipline.

"No power on earth," writes Dietrich Von Hildebrand,

> no temptation or attraction however potent, can force our assent; no pressure or influence can forcibly provoke our decision. Much can be imposed on man's body by violence. . . . he can be made to perform certain actions repugnant to him, and particularly, can be prevented from doing anything he wishes to do; but no matter what limitations are placed upon his outward sphere of action, nothing, except himself, has any power over his inward decision, over his ultimate, and irrevocably free, *Yes* or *No*.
>
> *Transformation in Christ*
> (Manchester, N.H.: Sophia Institute Press, 1990), 215

One who learned the folly of yielding tells her story.

"You feel so close. You almost 'melt' into one being, becoming physically intimate. It seems so right—almost. But way down deep a red warning light is flashing. You refuse to see it. Then you find you are both so aroused all else blacks out of your consciousness. Then it happens. You've gone too far. You've fornicated. The remorse is far, far deeper than the height of the excitement ever was.

"I know. I've been there. Oh, I know you may not get pregnant, although you live with that fear for some time. You may not get AIDS. Your boyfriend does not leave you and eventually you marry each other. But now there is always that gnawing, that big, dark, heavy cloud hanging over your marriage. It will always be there, even when you have repented and God has forgiven you. I know. I have grieved my Lord. I've been unfaithful to Him for the sake of a moment's selfish pleasure. From there on my life took a downward spiral into the depths of despair for many years. Yes, God has restored me. Yes, I am forgiven. Praise Him for His measureless love, grace, and faithfulness! Yet the cloud is always there."

One evening when her parents were not at home a girl invited her boyfriend over. It was not long before they found themselves in her bedroom and began to undress. Suddenly the boyfriend threw his clothes back on and went downstairs. When she came down, she said to him, "I've never been so proud of you!"

More often than we think, the other person may be reluctant to do wrong. When both suppose that the other expects intimacy, a very little resistance on the part of one may quickly turn the tide, to the relief of the other. We do not know how much hesitancy there may be and how glad the other person may be to be "let off the hook." Is a good-night kiss really wanted or is it merely expected? Perhaps at the very moment one is insisting on it, she is battling with her own conscience, entertaining a small hope that the man will have the moral fortitude to refuse.

In family prayers at home we used to sing a little gospel song that has been with me all my life and greatly comforted me in times of severe temptation.

Yield not to temptation, for yielding is sin.
Each victory will help you some other to win.
Fight manfully onward, dark passions subdue.
Look ever to Jesus, He'll carry you through.

Ask the Savior to help you,
Comfort, strengthen, and keep you.
He is willing to aid you—
He will carry you through.

H. R. Palmer

Reflections on "Temptation"

- Study Ephesians 4:22–24. Note the two selves. Which rules in your life?
- Name ways to *avoid* temptation.
- Name ways to *resist* temptation. The verse from 2 Timothy is one effective way.
- Remember the weapons we've been given.
- Would you take exception to Von Hildebrand's statement? Illustrate your answer.

26

Veins Running Fire

The fruit of the Spirit is . . . self-control.

Galatians 5:22

The awful struggle between spirit and flesh is best-known by those who believe that the difference between them is of very great importance. Mr. Rochester's agonized plea to Jane Eyre expresses that terrible conflict exactly.

"One instant, Jane. Give one glance to my horrible life when you are gone. All happiness will be torn away with you. What then is left? For a wife I have but the maniac upstairs. . . . What shall I do, Jane? . . ."

"Do as I do: trust God and yourself. Believe in heaven. . . ."

"Is it better to drive a fellow-creature to despair than transgress a mere human law? . . ."

This was true, and while he spoke my very conscience and reason turned traitors against me, and charged me with crime in resisting him. They spoke almost as loud as

Feeling: and that clamored wildly. "Oh, comply!" it said. "Think of his misery; think of his danger—look at his state when left alone; remember his headlong nature; consider the recklessness following on despair—soothe him; save him; tell him you love him and will be his. Who in the world cares for you? Or who will be injured by what you do?"

Still indomitable was the reply—"care for myself." The more solitary, the more friendless, the more unsustained I am, the more I will respect myself. I will keep the law given by God; sanctioned by man. I will hold to the principles received by me when I was sane, and not mad—as I am now. Laws and principles are not for the times when there is no temptation: they are for such moments as this, when body and soul rise in mutiny against their rigour; stringent are they; inviolate they shall be. If at my individual convenience I might break them, what would be their worth? They have a worth—so I have always believed; and if I cannot believe it now it is because I am insane— quite insane: with my veins running fire, and my heart beating faster than I can count its throbs. Preconceived opinions, foregone determinations, are all I have at this hour to stand by: there I plant my foot.

Lines must be drawn—*in advance.* "Foregone determinations" she called them. Principles. These establish guards in advance, destined to prevent us from faltering when our steadfastness may be put on trial.

Is there a man anywhere who would not prefer to have a virgin for a wife? A woman who would not prefer that the man she marries has never slept with anyone else? Where will these virgins be found?

Who should take the lead in a potentially explosive situation? Surely the one God created first is to be the initiator—initiating not intimacy but restraint. Too often, as in the case of Mr. Rochester and Jane, it is the man who urges intimacy, the woman restraint.

Among Christians today, intimacy begins where least expected—in discussing spiritual things. There should be a warning sign here: Dangerous Pothole. A man and woman meet in church, begin to converse, spend hours just talking, and find they have many affinities. They read the Bible together. They pray. Then comes "sharing," and spiritual intimacy soon turns to an emotional strip-tease. He probes. She spills her life story. He spills his. They tell each other how they feel about everything.

It is but a small step to sexual sin.

Foregone determinations may never have been thought of. All seemed so safe. They were just friends.

The restraint for which Jane Eyre fought is dismissed by many as quaint, ridiculous, and even impossible, but it is not only women who long for purity, as this heartening story illustrates.

Somewhere in Australia a boy in his early teens named Malcolm heard about a missionary who, in seeking to take the gospel to an Indian tribe, was murdered. That man's death, far from frightening the boy, only caused him to determine to follow Jesus Christ.

"His religious instruction teacher was the only Christian contact he had. His parents were not religious at all. But God prepared him for his commitment from an early age. There was a Bible encyclopedia at home which he read whenever he had a chance. He lived on a farm in a beautiful little country town. He would walk up to the top of the hill and just talk to the Lord for hours.

"In this encyclopedia was a picture of a boy kneeling down by his bed at night. Malcolm would wait till no one was looking, to avoid teasing, and then he would pray by his bed. He remembers, after hearing the missionary story, praying to God in the same way he was used to. Kneeling by his bed he said, 'They've killed some of Your children. You can have my life now. I want to live for you.'

"Just as simple as that.

"One day his oldest brother came home a changed man. Someone at work had led him to Christ. He came back to live at home so he could witness to his family. It was a pleasant surprise for him to find out that his introverted brother shared his new-found faith. Within the next few months they had the joy of seeing the rest of the family come to know the Lord!"

Far from Australia a Mexican mother from a peasant background was at the same time encouraging her daughter Amada and helping her to pray that she would be willing to wait before the Lord, to keep herself, including lips and hands, for the man God would give her as a husband. If marriage was not God's best for her, she prayed that her body would be kept pure in reverence to the Lord.

"One day someone I respected told me my way of thinking wasn't worth the effort," wrote Amada. "Why keep yourself when the guy you'll marry surely will have had half a dozen girlfriends before he decides to marry? Her advice was: Stop knocking dates back. You might as well enjoy it.

"I said to Mother, 'We didn't think about that one.' Her simple reply was, 'Let's ask the Lord to keep him just for you.' So we did.

"During my adolescence the Lord blessed me with some godly friends—boys who put God first and never took advantage of our friendships, girls who taught me and encouraged me to grow."

"One year after we moved to Australia this quiet, handsome, country boy asked me to marry him. I was twenty-two, Malcolm was thirty-two. His commitment to Christ remained unstained, inwardly and physically. I give witness with all my heart that our God is a faithful, loving God. It wasn't merely my prayers or Mother's prayers that brought this about, but God's GRACE. Mal was my first boyfriend, I was his first girlfriend."

Hearing this story, some high school girls were amazed to learn that such restraint is possible. The ecstasy of desire deferred was to them "a truly fabulous thing—if only we'd known this sooner!"

"I want my children to know this," wrote one of them. "Think of the immense pleasure of never having kissed anyone but the man you marry—what a wedding night!"

What is a kiss? Here is how one girl defined it: "A kiss to me is a contract, almost a seal of covenant. Friends who decided not to kiss until they reached the altar advise me that holding hands and kissing throughout their engagement would have 'whetted their appetites' too much. I don't hold these bits of advice as doctrine, but I'm excited that if or when the time comes for me to be swept into the sea of love, I'll have a sure and steady log to cling to."

A story in the Seattle *Times,* May 1992, is headed, "Don't Kiss This Off: Here's a couple who withstood the test of time." Natalie DeBusschere had called the newspaper with a very unusual gripe.

"My husband and I waited until we got married to kiss. What's weird is that people think we're weird for waiting that long. They think it's more weird for us to wait to kiss than to go out and have sex with someone on a one-night stand. They wondered if there was something wrong, maybe we were sexually incompatible, maybe the sparks just weren't there."

Natalie was twenty-one, Paul twenty-four, a medical student. Religion, they said, is the most important part of life. The columnist who wrote the article told Paul there would be a lot of men reading this who would marvel at his patience. "Devout Christian or not, most other men would have walked out."

They had met while doing volunteer work and joined in group socials before they went on a date. They dated six months, then were engaged for ten. Natalie told Paul she didn't believe in sex before marriage, and to make sure she didn't get carried away, she wouldn't kiss either, remembering the Bible's warning, "Can a man scoop fire into his lap without his clothes being burned?" (Prov. 6:27).

To Natalie kissing was that fire, but Paul pointed out that there might be a difference between kissing goodnight and "totally making out." Natalie said the no-kissing rule was where she felt comfortable drawing the line. She had seen what happened to the young women in her college dorm when they allowed men to stay the night.

"[Paul and Natalie] talked. You tend to talk much more if you're young and in love and not even kissing. . . . Paul said, 'It was just . . . plain . . . *tough.*'"

They were married on July 20, 1991. That first kiss, at the *altar*, took quite a while. Applause followed.

"Once I have determined where I will draw the line in a physical relationship," writes a woman who has a master's degree and a strong desire to be married, "how do I let a man I'm dating know where that line is? Do I wait till he tries something?"

Words should not be necessary. A woman's dignity and bearing, a certain mystery, will tell a true gentleman that she is a lady. He will treat her with respect and courtesy, which means hands off. But, sadly, too few women have learned how to be a lady, and even fewer men, it appears, have had any examples of true gentlemanliness that they can emulate. A little book entitled *Etiquette*, published in 1860, shows how unthinkable would have been a gentleman's touching a lady in any way at all without her permission.

It is the common custom in this country to shake hands on being introduced. This, however, should be optional with the person to whom you [a man] are presented, or with you, if you stood in the position of the superior. If a lady, or a superior in age or social position, offers the hand, you of course accept it cordially. You will have too much self-respect to be the first to extend the hand in such a case.

If a lady waltz with you, beware not to press her waist; you must only lightly touch it with the open palm of your hand, lest you leave a disagreeable impression not only on her *ceinture,* but on her mind.

There is something to be learned from these sensible old rules. Given today's earnest efforts to obscure the distinctions between the sexes (not to mention the careless freedoms encouraged even in churches, where everyone is asked to say to the one next to him, "God loves you and so do I"), the limits have been violated and highly inappropriate intimacies legitimized. I have been in churches where the congregation was very nearly forced not only to smile and hug but to massage their neighbor's neck and scratch his back. One who declines to capitulate to such foolishness is told that he needs to "lighten up." If physical contact with anybody and everybody is taken for granted, it is no wonder that a woman, even one with a master's degree, is unsure what to say and when.

Thank God for strong Christian men who honor the purity of their own bodies as well as the women's. They take the initiative in self-restraint and thus free women from anxiety. But because too many men have not been taught godly principles, women ask me to be very specific in matters that used to seem so self-evident and simple. I don't want to pontificate. I merely offer a few suggestions that have worked for me.

The first message you give will be your own reserve. "Keep them guessing," my mother said. "Don't give them anything to work on," my husband said. Keep a little space (arm's length is not always possible) between him and you. If he begins to close in, move ever so slightly in the opposite direction. If he has the temerity (and bad taste) to reach for your hand, gently pull away. If he casually throws an arm around you, the time has come for the second message, since he failed to read the first. This is a verbal one: "Please," or "Let's not do that," as you put a bit more distance between you. His response to any of these messages will tell you important things about what sort of man he is, and he will have perceived what sort of woman you are. Discussion is not necessary, and the subject of kissing or any other intimacy will not arise.

Are we to rule out all kisses, including the friendly peck-on-the-cheek greeting, and all hugs? I don't think so, but discretion is needed. Better to be too strict than too free. Even where everybody is kissing and hugging everybody, there is likely to be someone who hopes to find a special meaning in one person's greeting. Watch out.

The apostle Paul said that it is a good principle for a man not to have any physical contact with a woman (see 1 Cor. 7:1 *Phillips*). The word here translated "physical contact" means merely "to touch." Yet Paul also spoke of greeting one another with a *holy* kiss. An honest consideration of the difference, in the presence of God, will show us what is appropriate. If casual liaisons were common and dangerous in Paul's day, what of today? Are we made of different stuff? Yes, I suppose we are—we are much weaker and need much stronger rules.

An advice columnist in a *Christian* magazine suggested that any kiss over five *minutes* was "probably" too long. "I almost died when I read that," a girl wrote. "There is never any advice that requires someone to make a sacrifice!"

Flee from sexual immorality. All other sins a man commits are outside his body, but he who sins sexually sins against his own body. Do you not know that your body is a temple of the Holy Spirit, who is in you, whom you have received from God? You are not your own; you were bought at a price. Therefore honor God with your body.

1 Corinthians 6:18–20

If someone asks me, "Why shouldn't I touch, hold hands, kiss?" I ask, "Why should you?" The honest answer, of course, is "Because I enjoy it." The greater the enjoyment, the greater the risk. Should one then make physical contacts? The following questions will help with the answer.

Do I enjoy shaking hands with the minister at the church door in the same way that I enjoy holding hands with a member of the opposite sex who happens to be very attractive to me?

When I kiss my grandmother does it have exactly the same effect as kissing a pretty girl?

A touch that might become exciting is the beginning of sexual foreplay. This is the way God arranged things. Any such encounter may start the fire running in one's veins. Divine Wisdom purposed that one thing should lead to another. The act begins in thought. When the first touch occurs, momentum gathers.

I have found that a man will usually be as much of a gentleman as a lady requires, and probably no more.

Let both men and women take the question to God and decide in solitude what is the *right* course and what foregone determinations need to be made. Those who are determined to live in a way that pleases God will accept His instructions.

We beg and pray you by the Lord Jesus, that you continue to learn more and more of the life that pleases God, the sort of life we told you about before. You will remember the instructions we gave you then in the name of the Lord Jesus. God's plan is to make you holy, and that entails first of all a clean cut with sexual immorality. Every one of you should learn to control his body, keeping it pure and treating it with respect, and never regarding it as an instrument for self-gratification, as do pagans with no knowledge of God. . . . The calling of God is not to impurity but to the most thorough purity, and anyone who makes light of the matter is not making light of man's ruling but of God's command. It is not for nothing that the Spirit God gives us is called the *Holy* Spirit.

1 Thessalonians 4:1–8 *Phillips*

Reflections on "Veins Running Fire"

- Have you made some *foregone determinations?*
- Do you know a young person whom you could help to do the same?
- Is sexual purity primarily a women's issue? Explain your answer.
- It is heartening to find a young boy who has the moral fortitude to stand alone. What does it take to do that?
- Do you think people are more respectful of each other when they are called "men and women" or "guys and gals"? Or does it make any difference?
- In that very first encounter between a man and a woman in the Garden of Eden what do you imagine the dynamics to have been? What did they lose when they declared their independence of God?

27

Grace Greater
than All Our Sin

If we claim to be without sin, we deceive ourselves and
the truth is not in us. If we confess our sins, he is faithful
and just and will forgive us our sins and purify us from all
unrighteousness. If we claim we have not sinned, we make
him out to be a liar and his word has no place in our lives.

1 John 1:8–10

Bill's girlfriend went off to college and was taken in by a
fellow student who persuaded her that he had been given
a "word of knowledge"—she was to be his wife. Therefore, his argument ran, he had the rights of a husband over
her, including sex. In a few months he tired of her and she
saw him no more. Bill was devastated when he heard the
story, felt self-righteous and judgmental. Hadn't he deserved
a virgin? Against his own better judgment, Bill kissed her,
then "tried more than kissing," to which she said no. Now
he was resentful and bitter.

"I'm having such a hard time with forgiveness," he wrote.

A fifteen-year-old girl made up her mind to disobey God and her mother. She gave away her virginity. Her excuses: "Daddy didn't love me VERY much," and "everybody's doing it."

She now writes, "I was not a Christian at the time but I knew of God and knew in my heart that it was wrong, as Romans 1:20 says, I was 'without excuse.' The truth in God's eyes was that I had chosen to live in disobedience. I followed with several meaningless relationships until I met my husband, we became Christians by God's grace, and married.

"I am now thirty years old, married to a loving and God-fearing husband, and have three beautiful, healthy children. I am able to stay at home in a very little house, and it would appear that I have all the world at my fingertips. And yet fifteen years later this sin is a grievous weight on my heart. I had made a mistake I could never change.

"The more I study God's Word and the more I desire His presence in my life, the more I grieve over this sin. Just this past year I have begun to realize that the Father's calling for purity and holiness is for me. The Lord spoke to me through Hebrews 10:22, 23: 'Let us draw near to God with a sincere heart in full assurance of faith, having our hearts sprinkled to cleanse us from a guilty conscience, and having our bodies washed with pure water. Let us hold unswervingly to the hope we profess, for he who promised is faithful.'

"Is it possible? I wondered. Could the Lord not only forgive me, but cleanse my conscience and my body?

"My husband, knowing what I was dealing with, decided that we should separate physically for a time so that I could seek the Lord fully and be dealt with by His hand. So he moved into the guest room and was very patient and supportive, always ready to listen with love and forgiveness.

"My prayer for this time was Proverbs 20:27, 'The lamp of the Lord searches the spirit of a man; it searches out his inmost being.' I prayed that He would search my inmost being and reveal to me how I could receive the cleansing offered in Hebrews 10:10, 'we have been made holy through the sacrifice of the body of Jesus Christ once for all.' I wish I could say that it was an instant cleansing (which was actually what I was expecting!) but instead it was a slow, painful process. One by one the Lord revealed past sins and hurts that I had long since buried. The rejection of my father, the shame of a broken relationship, each revealed and each mourned over one at a time. Often the memories came in dreams, and I would wake up sobbing and broken. Many of my sins I knew I needed to confess to my husband, because I would never be able to feel completely loved by him unless he knew the ugly parts of me too. What a wonderful man—he was always much more willing to forgive me than I was to forgive myself.

"After weeks of cleansing, I reached a point of physical and emotional exhaustion. I was at my lowest, and began to pray that the Lord would bandage all my wounds before I bled to death! I remember telling one very dear friend that I felt like 'one great big open wound.' She opened her Bible and began to read to me from Isaiah 61.

> He has sent me to bind up the brokenhearted,
>> to proclaim freedom for the captives
>> and release from darkness for the prisoners, . . .
> to bestow on them a crown of beauty
>> instead of ashes,
> the oil of gladness
>> instead of mourning,
> and a garment of praise
>> instead of a spirit of despair. . . .
> They will . . . restore the places long devastated; . . .
> Instead of their shame

> my people will receive a double portion,
> and instead of disgrace
> they will rejoice in their inheritance;
> and so they will inherit a double portion in their land,
> and everlasting joy will be theirs.

"As she read to me, once again I began to weep, but instead of sadness, I was weeping with joy! This was the healing ointment that my aching heart needed. How loving and faithful our Lord is. Only He could change this dirty, ugly woman into beauty and joy. It was more than I had thought to ask for.

"It has only been a month since I was given this scripture, but my burden has been cast down at the foot of the cross, and I am learning how to stand up straight, without the stoop that carrying such a load has caused me. Does it still hurt? Yes. I still cannot read Isaiah 61 without crying. But I *have* been sprinkled from a guilty conscience and washed in pure water, and the One who promised me this *has* been found faithful.

"Why have I shared all this with you? I have trusted you with my heart, Elisabeth, to tell you this:

"Sexual immorality can be forgiven, but it causes pain like no other sin can (1 Cor. 6:18). I carried it around for fifteen years and as much as I wanted it to go away, it didn't. A girl's body and virginity are precious treasures, and when they are given away before marriage it is a painful mistake and can never be reclaimed. Anyone who says different *is a liar.* Please don't stop your plea to young people to guard carefully the trust God has given them."

Julia H. Johnston's lovely old hymn expresses the "marvelous grace of our loving Lord."

> Sin and despair like the sea waves cold
> Threaten the soul with infinite loss;

Grace that is greater, yes, grace untold
Points to the refuge, the Mighty Cross.

Another teenager who, by "sleeping around," squandered the one-time gift of virginity, began very seriously to walk with God when she reached her twenties.

"I thrill again and again as I realize the power of God to change lives so drastically. I dated a very exemplary Christian fellow. He proposed to me several times, and several times I declined, fearing engagement and marriage because I felt I could not tell my husband-to-be about my past, yet I felt it was wrong not to tell him. I would need his forgiveness, desperately, but I could not face the risk of not being forgiven, and, consequently, of being rejected. I cried many, many nights over this unchangeable status. One day in Bible college I was talking with my dorm mother with whom I was very close. She was so pleased and happy that I took such an interest in her nine-year-old daughter because she wanted her daughter to be around godly young people. I could not but cry. In the past, parents had told their kids to stay away from me, and here was a heroine of mine saying she was glad her daughter had the opportunity of being around me. My tears, of course, made her inquisitive, and tremblingly, I poured out my story to her. I told her my fears of telling a husband-to-be. She encouraged me to keep no secrets from my husband as keeping secrets would create a barrier in my marriage. She assured me that should God bring a young man into my life, then at the right time God would both give me courage to tell him and would pour out His grace on the young man so that he would readily forgive me. That idea sounded not only impossible but ridiculous!

"This summer I had a few dates with a young man in his thirties. I'm his first girlfriend. We committed to communicate. Little by little I revealed something of my past, keeping it all rather vague. I was torn between wanting him to pick up on my hints and wanting him to miss them altogether. He revealed his past, too—he had been a good kid!

"We became engaged in March, to be married in June. In April the 'right time' came. Bringing up my past seemed easy. It was late at night but he just sat at the kitchen table waiting patiently for me to talk until I had completely relieved my heart. He told me he had picked up the hints last summer. He was determined not to leave until I had told him as much as I wanted to tell him. I finally admitted to him that I was struggling with not knowing if he could forgive me if he knew that his arms were not the first to hold me, his kisses not my first kisses, and things that I should have been able to give him as 'firsts' I could not because they were already gone.

"He told me, 'I don't understand it myself, but somehow it doesn't matter to me, because I see what you are now, and I know what God has done in your life. You aren't what you used to be. I love you.' I finally got my courage up and asked if it didn't matter either if our first night would not be the first time. He said, 'I guess you expect me to say it does matter, but even that really doesn't. God has changed you. I still love you so much I want to marry you.'

"The grace of God is a wonderful thing, isn't it?

"Something has changed in our relationship. When he says, 'I love you,' it means more than it ever has before, and my telling him my whole heart thrilled him because he knows that I am really committed to doing everything I can, even if it is painful to me, to make our marriage the best I can.

"He stated that he is still looking forward to our first night as a very special time and wondered if I felt that our first night had lost the specialness. I replied that it has not lost all special meaning because he loves me, and the other guys really didn't. 'So,' he said, 'I am a first after all!'

"Isn't he sweet?"

Johnston's hymn continues:

> Dark is the stain that we cannot hide.
> What can avail to wash it away?
> Look! there is flowing a crimson tide.
> Whiter than snow you may be today.

A twenty-four-year-old, supposing she was the only virgin among her peers, gave herself to a man she thought was "safe enough."

"Little did I know that this sexual union would lead to years of miserable attachment to this man. I felt at times I needed to die in order to get away from him. I gave in to my fleshly desires with other men, deceiving myself into thinking it was okay to go out alone with Christian as well as non-Christian men. I allowed them into my apartment, allowed them to kiss and hug me. I know my limits, I told myself, I know how far I can go. I had not surrendered my passions to Christ—I was still in control, and my foolishness led to more sexual encounters and much grief.

"God graciously gave me the gift of repentance and I began to pray to be made pure again. I had my doubts. We tend to think that God is going to give us what we deserve, and we forget about His grace.

"Several months later God caused the head of a single man in my church to turn toward me. He cautiously began to make conversation with me, introduced me to his parents, maintained a certain distance. I, now wiser, followed his lead, but felt frustrated at the slow pace of the relationship—was he ever going to hold my hand? declare his feelings? God graciously gave me patience.

"The day came when he confessed his love for me and asked me to be his wife. We had never held hands or embraced, but we had come to know one another and knew that we wanted to spend the rest of our lives together, not because of sexual chemistry or physical attraction, but because of love and respect, and a regard for God working in our lives and bringing us together.

"God not only restored my sense of purity, He blessed me with a man that I couldn't even envision, let alone hope for. My husband was not only a virgin, he had never kissed a woman! It was too good to be true.

"God has allowed so much healing to come into my life because of the love of a man who purposed in his heart to remain pure. Although, sadly, I was promiscuous and 'used,' God's grace overruled that. I did not get what I deserved, but I received a wonderful gift. But why didn't God bless my husband with a virgin? I believe that He gave him instead a glorious opportunity to love his wife as Christ loves the church—not holding her sins against her, but accepting her and loving her unconditionally."

Nothing seems more miraculous, more difficult for us who insist on figuring things out, than this matter of grace. Logic has nothing to do with it. It is the incomprehensible and inscrutable High and Mighty One pouring Himself out in love for His helpless, sinning creatures. Through the sacrifice of Himself He offers us, when we ask for it, absolute forgiveness.

Nor does He merely forgive. He sanctifies us, definitively establishing a new quality of life in the cleansed soul, communicating to us *His* life and love, quite apart from any merit whatsoever on our side.

> Marvelous, infinite, matchless grace,
> freely bestowed on all who believe;
> You that are longing to see His face—
> Will you this moment His grace receive?

Grace, grace, God's grace,
Grace that will pardon and cleanse within;
Grace, grace, infinite grace,
Grace that is greater than all our sin.

Reflections on "Grace Greater than All Our Sin"

- Note the fruits of rebellion: virginity gone, fear, shame, conflict.

- Past experiences influence our lives positively and negatively. How many of our failures and sins ought we to excuse because of the negative experiences? Distinguish between excuses and reasons, then study Philippians 3:13–14.

- Do we choose to sin?

- The Bible states that "where sin increased, grace increased all the more" (Rom. 5:20). Shall we go on sinning, then, so that grace may increase? (See Romans 6:2.)

- Note the grace manifested in the husband of the second story: patience, understanding, love, forgiveness. (See Ephesians 5:25–27.) What evidence do you find of the wife's true repentance?

- The dorm mother advised a student to keep no secrets from her future husband. Would you take exception to this? If so, when and why? (Elizabeth Goudge's book, *The Rosemary Tree*, tells of one wife's decision to keep her secret. She believed it wrong to buy her own peace of mind at the cost of her husband's. Ponder that one.)

- Can you trust God for His clear guidance and obey Him when it comes? He leads His dear children in different paths, all of them paths of righteousness.

- Reflect: God does not restore virginity, but He will give purity and chastity to one who repents and prays for it.

28

Marriage:
A Right or a Gift?

The Lord God is a sun and shield;
the Lord bestows favor and honor;
no good thing does he withhold
from those whose walk is blameless.

Psalm 84:11

Lord, you have assigned me my portion and my
cup;
you have made my lot secure.

Psalm 16:5

If you are single today, the portion assigned to you for *today*
is singleness. It is God's gift. Singleness ought not to be viewed
as a problem, nor marriage as a right. God in His wisdom
and love grants either as a gift. An unmarried person has the
gift of singleness, not to be confused with the gift of *celibacy*.

When we speak of the "gift of celibacy," we usually refer to one who is bound by vows not to marry. If you are not so bound, what may be your portion tomorrow is not your business today. Today's business is trust in the living God who precisely measures out, day by day, each one's portion.

Do you care enough for the safety of the Everlasting Arms to yield yourself up to them, or, like a recalcitrant child, do you stiffen and cry, convinced that God has denied a legitimate claim? Do you see marriage as your birthright or as a gift to be granted or withheld?

As a single woman I had no question that it was man's responsibility to do the wooing. This meant holding back my natural aggressiveness and trusting God to work in the heart of a man—*if* marriage was in His plan for me. A man, on the other hand, has a different position. He too must learn to hold back his "hunter" instinct, praying, watching, and trusting God to show him what to do and when. When he is shown, he is to act, accepting the demands of his headship and the sacrifice that goes with it.

The story of Charles M. Alexander should encourage every godly man who begins to feel that he will never find the wife who measures up to his list of desired qualifications.

Alexander was a young soloist and song leader who traveled the world at the turn of the century with the famous evangelist R. A. Torrey. Years went by, and they were never long enough in one place for Charles to find the lady of his dreams.

"I had reserved the right in my mind to choose my own wife, and had decided that she must have this and the other qualities of mind and heart, but had never been able to find one who combined all the desired qualifications. During the Christmas season of 1903, which I was spending alone in London, I surrendered the whole matter to God, never dreaming that His answer would come so quickly, or that Birmingham would be the place where I should find my wife. During an afternoon meeting in Bingley Hall a week or two later, I noticed a young lady upon one of the platform seats. Immediately a feeling came over me that there was the answer to my prayer. I did not know who she was, but observed her closely, and grew to love her, for I saw that she was after the salvation of souls. I noticed that in the after-meetings she usually went down to the back of the Hall, and was not afraid to stay late, and work long and earnestly, sometimes with the most wretched-looking and poorly-clad women and girls. The more I saw of her, the more thoroughly I was convinced that, as far as I was concerned, she was my choice, though I was still asking the Lord constantly to take everything into His hands.

"I had noticed a silver-haired lady with her, evidently her mother. One day, early in the mission, this lady gave me an invitation to spend my rest-day at her home. I accepted, and after she had gone, I turned to some one and asked who the lady was. 'Why, that is Mrs. Richard Cadbury,' I was told. This was a surprise, as I had already visited the home of some of her relatives. It was not until the last rest-day of the mission that I, with several others of the mission staff, was entertained at Uffculme, her home. Strangely enough, and quite unknown to each other until afterwards, my future wife and I were praying earnestly on that same Friday night for the Lord's guidance in this matter. Each of us had a hard battle to fight with our own self-will, but each finally surrendered to the Lord, to have or not to have, as He should will.

"It was not until two days after the mission had closed that I spoke a word to Miss Cadbury about it, and then— why, it was all settled in a few minutes. We were on our knees almost as soon as I had spoken to her, thanking the Lord for bringing us together, and for the wonderful joy, which we took as a gift direct from Him."*

* From *Charles M. Alexander* by his wife (London: Marshall Bros. Ltd., n.d.— approx. 1921), 80ff.

To both Alexander and his future wife, when love was first confessed and accepted, the unmistakable leading of God was as clear as noonday. To them both, the revelation had come with a bewildering ecstasy of holy joy. Never before had either opened the sacred deeps of the heart, and when love came in floods of overwhelming force, they gratefully accepted it as from the hand of God.

A man who had read the above story was moving deliberately toward a proposal when he learned that the lady had deeply negative feelings about marriage. He was thankful to have been spared a great mistake. He wrote, "While I fully concur with you that the Lord is well able to lead pairs of His faithful children together precisely as He did the Alexanders, I wonder if we're justified in considering any deviations from it as departures from the Lord's will. In my case a lengthy period of communication or 'dating,' if you will, proved that my sense of God's leading was false."

I would see his sense of God's leading in this case not as false, but as He promised: "Along unfamiliar paths I will guide them" (Isa. 42:16). He does not give us a map or a preview. He simply tells us to follow Him. He's the Shepherd. A lamb who found himself in the Valley of the Shadow of Death might conclude that he had been falsely led. It was needful for him to traverse that darkness in order to learn not to fear. The Shepherd is still with him.

Those who long for the gift of marriage can find great peace in the words of Psalm 16:5, receiving *one day at a time* the divinely apportioned gift of singleness, believing that our Heavenly Father's love will withhold nothing that is *good* for us.

It should not be forgotten that a lifetime of singleness may be His choice for us. Will we still love Him, trust Him, and praise Him?

201

Reflections on "Marriage: A Right or a Gift?"

- Alexander's story illustrates principles worth studying.
    1. Surrender to the will of God.
    2. Be faithful in performance of duties.
    3. Expect God to guide.
    4. Be watchful as to that guidance.
    5. Set character as the priority.
    6. Commit natural feelings to God.
    7. Don't "date" but give a frank confession of love (this is the man's initiative).
    8. Recognize God's gift.

- Reflect on the "cup" given to us, according to Psalm 16:5. Then think of Jesus' total acceptance of the cup His Father gave Him: the cross. Remember His word to any who would follow Him: Take up your cross.

29

He Can Search My Girl among the Nations

The eyes of the LORD range throughout the earth to strengthen those whose hearts are fully committed to him.

2 Chronicles 16:9

Some who plan on being foreign missionaries are troubled, as was I, by the question of how one would ever meet the right husband or wife on the field, especially if the culture is one in which dating is unknown. It is a sovereign God whom we serve. If He leads us to the remotest jungle or steppe, we can safely follow, sure that He knows how to arrange those felicitous meetings we worry so much about.

We need to be reminded that dating is a very recent phenomenon. Most marriages in most of human history have occurred without anything remotely resembling the current American mode. When Abraham wanted a wife for his son Isaac he sent his trusted servant to find one. Assured that God would send an angel before him, the servant took an oath, loaded ten camels with gifts, and set out. He went to the one place where women could be observed with propriety—the town well at evening. Note what he did there:

He stood and prayed.

He watched the women as they came.

He knew that he himself must exercise judgment. He must choose one of the girls.

He then asked God to let the one *he* chose *be* the one *God* had chosen!

Before he'd said amen out came a beautiful virgin. I do not doubt that the man had an eye for beauty and for dress, by which he recognized her virginity.

When he asked her for a drink of water he observed that she was quick about it and went far beyond the usual courtesy in volunteering to water his ten camels.

"Without saying a word, the man watched her closely to learn whether or not the LORD had made his journey successful" (Gen. 24:21).

Here is a world of instruction: a man's obedience, prayer, judgment, and keen observation not only of physical beauty but also of strength of character. No wonder he bowed down and worshiped the Lord for His faithful guidance.

That servant's God is the same yesterday, today, and forever. He is still in the business of hearing prayer and guiding His people, as the following letter demonstrates.

"I'm glad to share my story about how God revealed and carried out His will for my marriage, to support your view of 'no date' before marriage.

"I'm an international student in America. I came here in August 1989. At the beginning of my study it was very tough for me. I had a lot of problems to overcome. At the end of that year, I read a book which drew my attention about having a family. But what interested me was the part of prayer in the end of this book. The author illustrated examples how children are encouraged and grow in faith when their prayers were heard and answered. It motivated me to pray serious prayer about my marriage and I laid my needs before the Lord.

"In the beginning of 1991 the revelation of God came to my heart—the story of Isaac and Rebekah. At that time I knew my girl might be someone I have never met or seen.

"For several months I was so joyful to receive His promise for me (God convinced me so many times), and I thanked Him for giving me a promise, even though I did not know who the girl was. Then it came—the real battle of my faith and the test of my patience to wait upon the Lord.

"During my summer vacation, I got plenty of time outside of my research. Most of the time I felt lonely, so I assumed that the Lord should present my girlfriend at that time, because I felt lonely. But the Lord seemed to delay His answer. I prayed earnestly day after day ever since the end of 1989 that He will present me the girl. But month after month, no answer. I became so impatient and anxious about it. The enemy tried every means to make me quit believing God's promise and search for the girl by myself. Sometimes I almost surrendered to the enemy. But due to God's grace and mercy, He reminded me of the story of Ishmael, the son of Abraham with Hagar who was not the will of God. It warned me that I would take the consequence and miss the blessings He ordained for me if I could not wait for His promise. Finally I surrendered my will to the Lord and decided to take *His* girl for me as my wife. I became so relieved, and peace and joy came back to me. But I still kept believing and praying in patience.

"One morning I felt so impressed to call my mom in my home country. This idea that she might know something about my marriage had been in my mind for several days. So I called her and asked her if she knew any Christian sister whom I can marry with (my mother is not a Christian). Immediately she replied her Christian friend had a daughter at the age of marriage. They would like us to know each other ever since I left for America. Due to the fact that they have been out of contact for one year my mom did not recognize their intention, so she had been hiding the story from me for one year at least.

"So I decided to pray and said to the Lord, 'Lord, if it is she, please keep the door open.' More exciting thing is yet to come: Guess where she was at that time? Brazil, a country so foreign to me, a country I have never thought of. Isn't God amazing. He can search my girl among the nations, among billions of girls and He knows which one is best for me.

"We have been keeping in touch and we know it is the will of God for us to marry. Without any hesitation we decided to marry each other before we met each other, not based upon what can be seen but on what the Lord said. In the winter of 1990 I traveled to Brazil to meet my bride-to-be and sensed God's presence strongly with me. Indeed she is a lovely and godly girl that I've been looking for. I want to thank God for His faithfulness.

"Dear Mrs. Elisabeth Elliot, I would like to witness for the Lord and offer my story to those singles who are feeling lonely to encourage them to trust the Lord until the end."

An American girl named Colleen believed that God had called her to foreign missionary work, although she could not imagine lasting very long at it unless she were given a husband. Committing that faithless objection to God she went off to Eastern Europe with the matter settled, "assuming I'd be single forever. I was *happy*, with such freedom and joy in serving Him."

The situation in which Colleen then found herself was a relatively safe one—a group of Christian men and women who were able to become friends (*"real* friends!" she said), knowing one another's views on crucial matters in a context of straightforward honesty. The best side and the worst side of each was public knowledge. Since the work often involved travel they discovered what others looked like the morning after sleeping in a van on the side of a road in Romania ("and *please* note that we *always* traveled in groups of three!").

Not surprisingly, one young man found himself more than ordinarily interested in one young woman. A wise and cautious man, he talked with several trusted older Christian friends, asking for their thoughts on whether to pursue a more serious relationship.

Colleen continues, "Following their positive response, and several months of prayer and seeking God's will, he simply asked me what I thought about the idea. Quite honestly, I was taken by surprise. I wasn't even thinking along this line. But Len was relieved when I said I was open to the idea and would pray about it. I believe strongly that the man should be the initiator but didn't realize until much later how difficult it is for a man to be turned down.

"We discussed openly and honestly what this would mean and concluded from the beginning that it would be a time of seeking whether God wanted us to marry. In our circumstances we felt that it would be pointless, and perhaps even detrimental to our ministry, not to be realistic from the beginning. It would definitely affect the course of our lives and even the direction of our ministry.

"Len felt we should move ahead, but willingly gave me 'space' and time to think and pray. We spent the next month apart (partly by choice, partly by the nature of our ministry), to avoid making an *emotional* decision.

"We also set a time limit so that the deciding wouldn't drag on forever, and in order to preserve our friendship if we decided that's all it was meant to be. For me this was an agonizing time because it seemed that the whole thing was boiling down to a calm, logical decision rather than one of feelings. I guess I had read too many stories about people falling madly in love and just 'knowing' that this was the right person.

"As I sat praying, reading God's Word, and making a list of pro's and con's, I felt God saying, 'Why not? Haven't you prayed for marriage, and isn't this the kind of man you've prayed for?'

"So we began to 'date' (isn't there a better word?). Len was marvelous about this. There was never any confusion about the status of our relationship. We still had many good times together with friends, and also independent of each other. But he made sure that a date was a date. He did the asking, the planning, and the paying. He opened doors, and was courteous in every way. This was something I had noticed before—a trait uncommon in today's men.

"It was during this time, as I began to look at Len with the thought 'Could I marry this guy?' that I fell in love with him.

"We agreed at the beginning that sex belongs in marriage. We set definite limits. Now you might think that living in a dormitory with a bunch of other missionaries would certainly not lend itself to much time alone. But lest you think that our waiting for sex until marriage was easy, let me tell you otherwise! No matter how impossible the situation, there were times when we found ourselves alone (and as you grow closer, you begin to seek out those times!). We were forced time and time again to say consciously,

'No. Not yet.' It was anything but easy, yet I can't stress enough that it was worth it!

"After about four months of dating, my parents visited us in Austria. I can see now God's hand in the timing—this visit was planned before they knew about Len! They enjoyed getting to know him and were great about including him in our plans. At a castle in Budapest overlooking the Danube River, Len asked my dad for permission to marry me, while my mom and I talked about the possibility, knowing that's surely what they were talking about. Len's mom then joined us from Hamburg, Germany, for a few days. A few days after my parents left, Len took me to a scenic lake near Berlin. We sat on a park bench, he got down on one knee, and asked, 'Will you marry me?' Although I had not known that this was the day, I knew the answer was yes. He put the engagement ring on my finger, kissed me, and said for the *first* time, 'I love you.'

"Now I'm learning to live with the reality of who this man is that I've married, or more accurately, *Whose* this man is! First and foremost, he belongs to God. I hadn't thought of all this would mean: moving, packing, and unpacking, living in another culture indefinitely, leaving family and friends. I'll admit there are times when I would like the security of a predictable income and a 'normal' family life. But I married a missionary, and I'm committed to go where he goes. It's when he's where God wants him to be that he's happiest, and I'm finding that too. When I consider the alternatives, it's worth it all. I guess I would tell Christian women seeking marriage, 'Watch out! You may get what you pray for! Be willing to make the sacrifices your husband may demand.' Once you've got him, he is not going to suddenly conform to your idea of marriage. His first priority is being obedient to God's calling. If God calls the husband, He calls the wife too."

Reflections on "He Can Search My Girl among the Nations"

- Study carefully the two things the servant did at the well: prayed and watched quietly. What did he watch for? How long did it take to assess the girl's *character?* What sorts of things nowadays reveal character—in women and in men? Where might one have opportunity to observe that?
- A lonely foreigner seeks the will of God. He puts himself in communication with God by prayer and careful study of the Bible. He brings a specific request.
- He finds instruction in the story of how Abraham found a wife for his son Isaac (Genesis 24) and takes this as God's promise that He will find a wife for him. This was an act of faith.
- The test of patience follows.
- The Adversary tempts him to take things into his own hands. He finds a warning against this in the story of Ishmael (Genesis 16).
- He surrenders his own will and desire to the Lord.
- He looks to his mother for help.
- Are dating and intimacy prerequisites to a happy marriage?
- Colleen and Len observe each other in a safe environment. They look and listen. Len asks advice.
- There is clarity from the start: marriage was the issue.
- They impose on themselves the discipline of a month apart, to think and pray.
- They set a time limit.
- A date was a date. No ambiguity.
- They recognize the need for self-control and willingness to sacrifice.
- Len asks her father's permission. Three parents are involved.

30

Love Means Sacrifice

If anyone comes to me and does not hate his father and mother, his wife and children, his brothers and sisters—yes, even his own life—he cannot be my disciple. And anyone who does not carry his cross and follow me cannot be my disciple.

Any of you who does not give up everything he has cannot be my disciple.

Luke 14:26, 33

On June 28, 1810, Nancy Hasseltine, age twenty-one, was at home in Bradford, Massachusetts. It was a large comfortable house that stood facing north across the Merrimack River. A prospective missionary named Adoniram Judson, age twenty-two, came for dinner.

"A table had been set in the west front room. As the guests filed in, . . . Adoniram noticed a girl . . . bent over a huge pie which she was cutting into generous slices. Instantly he decided she was the most beautiful creature he had ever seen. Her jet-black curls, clear olive complexion and dark, lustrous eyes would have made her appearance striking in any case. But there was something about the irrepressible smile lurking on the full curve of her lips—a certain gay impertinence, almost, in her dancing eyes—that hinted a vivacity and even mischievousness, under the conventional demureness, that were new and attractive to Adoniram. He had never seen a girl like her.

"He was anything but shy, yet when Parson Allen introduced him and she looked him full in the face, he was struck dumb. From then on he was extraordinarily aware of every move she made about the room as she served the guests, but he was unable to unglue his eyes from his plate. He could hardly make an intelligent reply when he was asked a question about the missionary movement at the Seminary. Perhaps, thought his questioners kindly, the young man was intimidated by the august gathering he was about to address. The truth was that, instead of thinking about the memorial in his pocket, he was preoccupied with the phrasing of a poem which kept composing itself, almost against his will, to this raven-haired beauty. . . .

"Nancy had heard of Adoniram Judson and the storm he had been stirring up in ecclesiastical circles, and had been curious to see what he looked like. And now that she saw him she was disappointed. He was fairly good-looking, of course, but perhaps a little too short and slight. His nose was somewhat too prominent, although that curly chestnut hair was rather attractive. And above all, where were the wit and liveliness she had heard about? His replies were nothing but abstracted monosyllables. Most of the time he spent staring into his plate. When the meal was over and young Mr. Judson mumbled his thanks and went out the door, she wondered why everybody made such a fuss about him. . . .

"One month from the day he met her he formally 'commenced an acquaintanceship' with her, which meant that he formally declared his intentions as a suitor. This he did in a letter, and tradition declares that for several days she did not reply. Its contents were an open secret within the Hasseltine family, however, so much so that one of her sisters finally threatened to answer the letter herself if Nancy delayed any longer.

"Her reply was not encouraging, but neither was it a flat rejection. Evading the issue, she wrote that her parents would have to consent before she could even consider Adoniram. Privately, she speculated in her journal whether she would be able to commit herself 'entirely to God' to be disposed of, according to His pleasure, and decided, 'Yes, I feel willing to be placed in this situation, in which I can do most good, though it were to carry the Gospel to the distant benighted heathen.'

"Adoniram promptly sat down at his table and wrote to Nancy's father:

> I have now to ask, whether you can consent to part with your daughter early next spring, to see her no more in this world; whether you can consent to her departure, and her subjection to the hardships and sufferings of a missionary life; whether you can consent to her exposure to the dangers of the ocean; to the fatal influence of the southern climate of India; to every kind of want and distress; to degradation, insult, persecution, and perhaps a violent death. Can you consent to all this, for the sake of Him who left His heavenly home, and died for her and for you; for the sake of perishing immortal souls; for the sake of Zion, and the glory of God? Can you consent to all this, in hope of soon meeting your daughter in the world of glory, with the crown of righteousness, brightened with the acclamations of praise which shall redound to her Savior from heathens saved, through her means, from eternal woe and despair?

"John Hasseltine . . . with many misgivings left it to Nancy to make up her own mind. Whatever her choice, she had his blessing—but let her consider carefully before taking an irrevocable action. Nancy's mother had little to add to this advice. She hoped Nancy would not go. But she would not withhold her consent. Thrown back on herself, Nancy did not know what to do. She was beginning to love Adoniram—what woman could withstand such a combination of impetuosity and tenderness?—and there must have been something irresistibly appealing about sharing his adventures in far places. But the hazards were appalling."

In September Nancy wrote to a friend:

> I feel willing, and expect, if nothing in providence prevents, to spend my days in this world in heathen lands. Yes, Lydia, I have about come to the determination to give up all my comforts and enjoyments here, sacrifice my affection to relatives and friends, and go where God, in His providence, shall see fit to place me. . . .
>
> Nor were my determinations formed in consequence of an attachment to an earthly object; but with a sense of obligations to God, and with a full conviction of its being a call in providence, and consequently my duty.

There is no record of precisely when she said yes to Adoniram, but by mid-October the word was out that she was to marry him.

"'Why does she go?' someone asked.

"'Why, she thinks it her duty. Would you not go if you thought it your duty?'

"'But I would *not* think it my duty.' . . .

"In her secret heart Nancy still sometimes found her determination undermined by fears.

> Jesus is faithful; His promises are precious. Were it not for these considerations, I should, with my present prospects, sink down in despair, especially as no female has, to my knowledge, ever left the shores of America to spend her life among the heathen; nor do I yet know, that I shall

214

have a single female companion. But God is my witness, that I have not dared to decline the offer that has been made me, though so many are ready to call it a wild, romantic undertaking.

It was more than a year before the two could begin their "wild, romantic undertaking," and they saw nothing of each other for most of that time.

On New Year's Day, 1811, Adoniram wrote to his beloved:

It is with the utmost sincerity, and with my whole heart, that I wish you, my love, a happy new year. May it be a year in which your walk will be close with God; your frame calm and serene; and the road that leads you to the Lamb marked with purer light. May it be a year in which you will have more largely the spirit of Christ, be praised above sublunary things, and be willing to be disposed of in this world just as God shall please. As every moment of the year will bring you nearer to the end of your pilgrimage, may it bring you nearer to God, and find you more prepared to hail the messenger of death as a deliverer and friend. And now, since I have begun to wish, I will go on. May this be the year in which you change your name; in which you take final leave of your relatives and native land; in which you will cross the wide ocean, and dwell on the other side of the world, among a heathen people.

He married her on February 5, 1812, and they sailed from Salem, Massachusetts, for Burma, along with another couple, on February 18—the first foreign missionaries to leave the shores of America.*

Since Adoniram's letter of proposal is lost, perhaps another man's letter, of the same era (1817), will give the flavor of what Adoniram's might have said. Note that the

* From Courtney Anderson, *To the Golden Shore* (Grand Rapids: Zondervan, 1972), 77–85.

question Will you marry me? is never asked. The writer was my great-great grandfather, Gurdon Trumbull, of Stonington, Connecticut, the recipient Sally Ann Swan.

Be not offended, Sally Ann, should the manner of this application be inconsistent with your idea of propriety. Was I conscious of its being so I should never have attempted it. My reasons for adopting this mode of communicating sentiments to you was to give you an opportunity of deciding without embarrassment and to learn your sentiments without a direct avowal. I hope that you will not be surprised at my declaration that a determination to make this attempt has been formed for more than two years and at no time have I ceased to look forward in hope to the period when I could with propriety adopt it. To you it is now referred, and your decision will either extinguish the last ray of hope or change it to reality, where I cannot hope for more. I cannot presume you unconscious of the sentiments of Regards which I have entertained toward you although not directly expressed, but if I am mistaken in this supposition believe me when I avow it now—actuated by sincere Esteem and well tested affection do I ask you to receive my addresses, directly and personally with the approbation of your Parents to whom I only wait your Permission to apply. I expect candor from you, and fear not that you will trifle with my Feelings: if your Heart absolutely decides against my pretensions I have nothing to hope from the application, and I only ask that this note may be returned in the same manner in which you receive it. This will effectually preclude all further importunity; if it is retained I shall feel myself authorized to hope for eventual success, and if the Book [of poems by Lucius M. Sargent, *Hubert and Ellen* (Boston, 1815)] is returned without the Note I shall consider it as an Evidence that I may expect your approbation in making direct and honorable proposals. I have no argument to urge in my Favor. I am too well known to you to expect success from deceitful pretensions. With anxiety shall I wait the result of this communication. If it is favorable can you doubt that I shall be happy in the gratification of the first wish of my Heart; if the Reverse, I must always Respect and Esteem you although I may be constrained to suppress more tender Emotions.

Relying on your Goodness to make painful suspense as short with me as possible,
I am with sincerity,
Yours,
Gurdon Trumbull

Reflections on "Love Means Sacrifice"

- Adoniram's intentions as a suitor are formally declared.
- Nancy insists on her parents' first consenting.
- He writes to them—a realistic forecast of missionary life.
- Albeit with misgivings, the parents leave the decision with Nancy.
- Convinced, in spite of fears, that this is God's will, she does not dare to decline.
- Trumbull's letter is less threatening than a meeting would be.
- He deliberates for two years before writing.
- He recognizes the need for her parents' consent.
- He sees her as a woman of integrity who will not trifle with his feelings.
- He furnishes an easy way for her to reply.
- He never asks her to marry him!

31

Do Not Be like the Horse

I will instruct you and teach you in the way you should
    go;
    I will counsel you and watch over you.
Do not be like the horse or the mule,
    which have no understanding
but must be controlled by bit and bridle
    or they will not come to you.
Many are the woes of the wicked,
    but the Lord's unfailing love
    surrounds the man who trusts in him.

Psalm 32:8–11

A story that appeared in my book *The Path of Loneliness* was
that of a heartbroken girl who had just parted with the
man she loved. To her surprise, it was not the end of the
world. She wrote several years later: "I thought you would
appreciate hearing from someone whom God has led

through the desert to the other side. Five years ago a large part of me was *very* close to despair. I grieved simultaneously over the loss of him and the dream of marriage and children. God has since healed and restored my joy in *Him,* my First Love. He made me whole by bringing me face-to-face with roots of bitterness and resentment so I could sacrifice them to Him (sound familiar?).

"I came closer and closer to thirty, and praying with faith became harder and harder. The *longing* I had for a godly man was indescribably intense, but in God's perfect time, His sovereign will began to take shape before my eyes. This gentle, kind, caring man whom I had noticed at church began to show me favor and then initiated a one-to-one relationship with me. Without reservation he made his intentions known from the first. He 'courted' me by being assertive and yet completely gentlemanly. He told me he had prayed about approaching me, that he had submitted "us" to God despite his own desires, and that he *wanted* to commit to a wife and children.

"It gives me great joy to tell you that on June 1 I will be married to the one I have waited on God for (not very patiently sometimes) and prayed for so long. I feel so secure in his love and the priority I have in his life. Mark is romantic and esteems my femininity. He is a true giver and does it subtly for another's edification, not for pats on the back. It's easy to love, respect, and admire a man who is God's, who lays down his life, as Jesus did, without a word. Mark is not perfect, but I am convinced he is God's choice, God's best, for *me.* How can one adequately thank Him for this kind of gift?

"Several of my youth group girls, now in college, ask me how I knew he was *the one.* I tell them about my Father, His promises of guidance, His love, and His sovereign wisdom. I also give them pages 47, 48 in *Passion and Purity* (which include references: Proverbs 14:12, 13; 1 Peter 5:7; Phil. 4:6; and Matt. 6:25).

"God really spoke to me through those pages as I was laying before Him this awesome decision to marry Mark. I did not want to marry outside of His will if He intended me to be single in order to serve Him better. I struggled over that and sought His *will,* not just His blessing."

And here is the tale of a *man's* patience, told by his wife.

"Seven years ago I asked you if it was o.k. to hope as you had that the Lord would bring you and Jim together. Wouldn't that be setting yourself up for heartbreak? You shared how, as children, we may ask for anything and hope for anything our heart desires. But we do so always with the understanding that our Father knows what's best and sees beyond what we see. When we hope it is always with the 'fine print' in which we acknowledge that we at times don't know what to ask for, don't know if what we hope for is right and good. So we leave the decision to Him, knowing He will do whatever is truly best for us.

"Several years later I met a young man, and as our relationship became more serious I read *Passion and Purity* several times, not really wanting to set such high standards, or rather, *wanting* to but not *really!* The Lord seemed to be opening all the doors to allow my friendship with Kevin to deepen. He was charming, persuasive, and experienced in the ways of women, but I held out for six months before I let him kiss me. He had said he loved me and we were both convinced this was *it.* I wrote to you several times and you cautioned me not to make any plans until the ring was on my finger. At the time I was preparing to go for a two-year term as a missionary. I planned to come back and get engaged to Kevin. I thought your advice was too cautious—after all, we loved each other! But that intimacy we shared in the physical clouded my perspective and confused the whole issue.

"After only three short months of my being overseas our relationship came unglued and fell apart. I was devastated, my heart was shattered. I wrote to you and you offered the comfort of the fact that I now had 'something new to offer'—a broken heart. I offered it to God.

"I felt so wounded I was sure I'd never heal, never love anyone like that again, I was wounded for life. Then I heard a tape which said it was a lie of the enemy to believe that some event that had happened would prevent something else from ever happening. As if a mistake you or someone else made would forever prevent God's will for your life.

"In England I met a nice young man from South Carolina named Rob who, when I got back to the States, invited me to join him for a lunch appointment with a guy he did not know but one whom some friends wanted him to meet. I declined, saying I'd rather stay in the library and write some letters. So Rob went off to lunch. About an hour later he walked into the library followed by a very handsome young man named David. David and I hit it off right away.

"From that day on he pursued me with much determination and creativity. Later he told me that during lunch with Rob they had discussed where they might find a suitable wife and Rob told him all about me. He was so intrigued he left lunch immediately so he could meet me. David tells me he knew in the first five minutes that I was the girl he'd waited his whole life to meet.

"As unreal as it may sound, David had *never dated* any other girl. After the heartbreak with Kevin I was convinced that *if* I was to marry, the Lord would have to make it clear to the guy for I was not going to make a single move. I reasoned that since I was only interested in marrying a godly man, then I could trust God to lead *him* to *me,* for he would be a man attuned to God's voice and would know that God was directing him to pursue me. This is exactly what happened. How faithful our Father is! He arranged all the details to bring us together.

"On March 16 David and I are to be married, Lord willing. How I praise God for protecting me from making a big mistake in marrying Kevin. The Lord protects us from ourselves. I really thought *I* knew what was best but the Lord so arranged things as to save me for David, who is so perfectly suited to me.

"P.S. The first time David will kiss me will be at the altar on our wedding day."

Reflections on "Do Not Be like the Horse"

- Bitterness and resentment over the prospect of singleness—confessed and sacrificed.
- A man's intentions made clear from the beginning.
- Prayer for what we desire—always footnoted by "Thy will be done."
- "No plans till the ring is on the finger"—too cautious?
- A broken heart: something to offer (Ps. 51:17).
- Intimacy clouding perspective.

32

He Had Begotten
an Affection in Her

Give me understanding, and I will keep your law
and obey it with all my heart.
Direct me in the path of your commands,
for there I find delight.

Psalm 119:34–35

George Muller is well-known throughout the world for
his orphanages in England, founded and sustained by faithful prayer. Prayer was the key to his life. On December 31,
1867, for example, he recorded: "During this year the Lord
has been pleased to give me £1,847 19s 4½ d.

"Notice particularly, esteemed reader, that it was not
only one year or another, and these far between, that I
was bountifully supplied by the Lord; but year after year.
Observe, also, in particular, that these donations were
received from hundreds of donors, who were residing not
only in various parts of England, Scotland, and Ireland,

but in France, Switzerland, Italy, Germany, Denmark, Sweden, Holland, Belgium, Canada, the United States, India, Australia, New Zealand, China, etc. There is scarcely a country in the world from whence I have not received donations for myself as well as for the Scriptural Knowledge Institution, which furnishes another precious proof that the hearts of all men are in the hands of God, and that, it we have Him on our side, we cannot but be cared for and helped, whatever our position may be, and wherever our lot may be cast."

In the year 1868, Muller received more than six times as much as he needed for himself and his family, "to have not only all the necessaries but all the conveniences of life!"

Not the least of the things that God had judged to be "necessaries" for George Muller had been His gift of a holy wife. On February 6, 1870, he wrote: "On October 7th, 1830, therefore thirty-nine years and four months ago, the Lord gave me my most valuable, lovely, and holy wife. Her value to me, and the blessing God made her to be to me, is beyond description. This blessing was continued to me till this day, when this afternoon, about four o'clock, the Lord took her to Himself.

"February 11. Today the earthly remains of my precious wife were laid in the grave. Many thousands of persons showed the deepest sympathy. About twelve hundred of the Orphans, who were able to walk, followed in the procession; the whole staff of Helpers at the Orphan-Houses who could be spared, and hundreds of believers of the Church with which she had been in communion; I, myself, sustained by the Lord to the utmost, performed the service at the chapel and in the cemetery."

His text was Psalm 119:68, "You are good, and what you do is good; teach me your decrees." Here is an edited version of the first half of his sermon.

"When it pleased God to take my darling wife to Himself, my soul was sustained by the words of my text. I desire now, as God may help me, for the benefit of my younger fellow-believers in Christ particularly, to dwell on the truth contained in these words:

I. The Lord was good, and did good, *in giving her to me.*
II. He was good, and did good *in so long leaving her to me.*
III. He was good, and did good, *in taking her from me.*

"I. *In giving her to me* I own the hand of God. When, at the end of the year 1829, I left London to labor in Devonshire in the Gospel, a brother in the Lord gave to me a card containing the address of a well-known Christian lady, Miss Paget, in order that I should call on her. For three weeks I carried this card in my pocket, but at last was led to make the effort to see her. Miss Paget asked me to preach in the room which she had fitted up at Poltimore, a village near Exeter. I accepted readily the invitation. She gave me the address of Mr. Hake, a Christian brother who had an Infant Boarding School in order that I might stay there. To this place I went at the appointed time. Miss Groves, afterwards my beloved wife, was there. This occasion led to others. Thus I went, week after week, to Exeter, each time staying in that house.

"All this time my purpose had been not to marry at all, but to remain free for traveling about in the service of the Gospel; but after some months I saw, for many reasons, that it was better for me, as a young Pastor, under twenty-five years of age, to be married. The question now was, to whom shall I be united? Miss Groves came before my mind; but the prayerful conflict was long before I came to a decision, for I could not bear the thought that I should take away from Mr. Hake his valued helper, as Mrs. Hake continued still unable to take the responsibility of so large a household. But I prayed again and again.

"At last this decided me: I had reason to believe that I had begotten an affection in the heart of Miss Groves for me, and that therefore I ought to make a proposal of marriage to her, however unkindly I might appear to act to my dear friend and brother, Mr. Hake, and to ask God to give him a suitable helper to succeed Miss Groves. On August 15, 1830, I therefore wrote to her, proposing to her to become my wife, and on August 19, when I went over as usual to Exeter for preaching, she accepted me. The first thing we did, after I was accepted, was to fall on our knees, and to ask the blessing of the Lord on our intended union.

"In about two or three weeks, the Lord, in answer to prayer, found an individual who seemed suitable to act as housekeeper, while Mrs. Hake continued ill; and on October 7, 1830, we were united in marriage. Our marriage was of the utmost simple character. We walked to church, had no wedding breakfast, but in the afternoon had a meeting of Christian friends in Mr. Hake's house, and commemorated the Lord's death; and then I drove off in the stage-coach with my beloved bride to Teignmouth, and the next day we went to work for the Lord.

"Now see the hand of God in giving me my dearest wife: (1) That address of Miss Paget's was given to me under the ordering of God. (2) I must at last be made to call on her, though I had long delayed it. (3) She might have provided a resting-place with some other Christian friend, where I should not have seen Miss Groves. (4) My mind might have at last, after all, decided not to make a proposal to her; but God settled the matter thus in speaking to me through my conscience—you know that you have begotten affection in the heart of this Christian sister, by the way you have acted towards her, and therefore, painful though it may be, to appear to act unkindly towards your friend and brother, Mr. Hake, you ought to make her a proposal. I obeyed. I wrote the letter in which I made the proposal, and nothing but one even stream of blessing has been the result. I think it is plain, that He who *'is good and doeth good'* had given me Miss Groves for a wife.

"Now let us see for a few moments what I had received in her as God's gift. I mention here as her chief excellence that she was a truly devoted Christian. She had for her one object of life to live for God; and during the thirty-nine years and four months that I was united to her, her steady purpose to live for God increased more and more.

"She was also, as a Christian, of a meek and quiet spirit. If all Christians were like her, the joys of heaven would be found on earth far more abundantly than they are now. Never at any time did she hinder me in the ways of God, but sought to strengthen my hands in Him, even in the deepest trials, under the greatest difficulties, and when the service in which she helped me brought on her the greatest personal sacrifices. When, during the years from September, 1838, to the end of 1846, we had the greatest trials of faith in the Orphan Work; and when hundreds of times the necessities of the Orphans could only be met by our means, and when often all our own money had to be expended, that precious wife never found fault with me, but heartily joined me in prayer for help from God, and with me looked out for help, and help came; and then we rejoiced together, and often wept for joy together.

"But the precious wife, who was God's own gift to me, was exquisitely suited to me, even naturally, by her temperament. Thousands of times I said to her, 'My darling, God Himself singled you out for me, as the most suitable wife I could possibly wish to have had.' Thousands of times I told her, 'My darling, I never saw you at any time since you became my wife, without my being delighted to see you.' This was not only our way in the first year of our marriage union, nor in the tenth, in the twentieth, and in the thirtieth year, but also in the fortieth year of our conjugal life. Thus I spoke to her many times since the seventh of

227

October, 1869. Further, day after day, if anyhow it could be done, I spent after dinner twenty minutes or half an hour with her in her room at the Orphan Houses, seated on her couch, which a Christian brother had sent her when she was ill. I knew it was good for her that her dear active mind and hands should have rest, and I knew well that this would not be, except her husband was by her side. There we sat, side by side, her hand in mine, as an habitual thing, having a few words of loving intercourse, or being silent, most happy in the Lord and in each other.

"We had not *some* happy days every year, nor a *month* of happiness every year—we had twelve months of happiness in the year, and thus year after year. Often and often did I say to that beloved one, and this again and again even in the fortieth year of our conjugal union, 'My darling, do you think there is a couple in Bristol, or in all the world, happier than we are?'"

Reflections on "He Had Begotten an Affection in Her"

- Note Muller's willingness to remain single in order to be free to serve God.
- He saw good reasons for a young pastor to be married.
- He wanted God to do the choosing.
- As he prayed, "Miss Groves came before" his mind. He was *listening.* Is it reasonable to expect God to answer in this way?
- How did God speak to Muller through his conscience? What did He say?
- Muller then saw a proposal as his *duty.*
- Do you find the happiness he describes incredible? (See John 15:10, 11.)

33

An Arranged Marriage

Honor your father and your mother, so that you may live long in the land the Lᴏʀᴅ your God is giving you.

Exodus 20:12

Dr. Ivy George, a diminutive and stunningly beautiful Indian woman, is professor of sociology in Massachusetts. In keeping with the custom of her country her parents had expected to arrange her marriage, a method most Westerners think ridiculous if not outrageous. Dr. George's story has much to teach us.

"August 5, 1977
"Dear Diary:
"Today I accepted Mummy's ultimatum that if I didn't get my visa at the U.S. Consulate next week, I would oblige the family by marrying the officer in the Navy. Word just came back today from his family that they are open to their son's marriage to me if I am willing.

"This is not the first time I've been in this place. All the men and their families were agreeable. I have been the one who has been 'adamant.' But this may be the last time I can stall for time. The market of men is getting scarce and my parents are getting tired. I must leave or marry, evacuate or be taken prisoner.

"Please, God, let this cup pass. Ivy.

"The cup passed. Within a week of the above entry I was granted permission to come to the U.S. I left with a smirk for all the men who wanted my hand and all the families who wanted my consent. Actually, it wasn't as triumphant as I make it sound. My entire life was bisected by that single act of departure, marking my time before and after. I was a very young woman then, barely having stepped onto the doorsill of womanhood.

"For the decade preceding this time I had been fed a steady diet of the Harlequin variety of romance, British style—Barbara Cartland, Hermina Black, Denise Robins, and the endless staples of strawberries, kisses, and summer wine, churned out of the Mills and Boon series.

"There was not much excitement to the marriages of our own families. My parents saw each other in the company of their families for twenty minutes prior to their wedding day. My friend Sheila had been betrothed to her maternal uncle ever since she was an infant. My brother and wife affirmed each other in holy matrimony after spending six hours with each other. Others, who chose to exercise some degree of individuality and independence, experienced ostracism in their communities. Such permutations were arranged in order to preserve property, lineage, and status.

"I was going to fight for my life before I succumbed to this fossilized idea of surrendering to a stranger forever. The fantasies spun by Robins, Black, and Cartland were far more appealing to me than the sterile and insipid marriages my friends were entering into at that time. But what if these romances were the stuff of someone's peculiar fantasies in order to sell her books and that was all? Yet, I said to myself, there was something special about being sought out for the self that one possessed. I wanted to know and be known, to become the subject of someone's desires.

"I hung on. My fears began to overcome me as I saw the faces of recently married young women, devoid of any *joie de vivre*, whose lives underwent traumatic transformation. As I saw the faces of those who were being primed and preened for this event, young girls full of verve and vigor, with dreams and schemes, confident of blazing a trail, I thought *Alas!* The past snagged their futures and lives came to naught. Images of cattle in a slaughter house haunted me. My heart ached for all of them, and my own status and stance towards marriage drew from them condescension at best, condemnation at worst.

"I spent my days in dissonance and disillusionment, puzzled at the chasm between the values extolled in other cultures and the dictates of my own.

"Families had arranged marriages since time immemorial and the system was particularly fail-safe in the face of the aggressive onslaught of Western culture that all urban Indian populations were faced with. While Western educated sons and daughters were additional bargaining chips in the marriage market, communal ties and family status superseded all that. For most of us, there was only one path, a well-worn one. Life was incomplete without a husband. No man, no identity. We were reminded of the occasional deviant who *chose* her own spouse—the result was disownment, disappearance, divorce, and in some cases death by suicide. Who would inflict such shame and scandal to self and family?

"I had the unusual privilege of having a mother who worked outside the home as a role model, so discussions of politics and world events were frequent in our home. She was fascinated by the movement of history and the power of literature, and often astounded visitors with her recitations and narratives. She taught my brother and me what she knew. Knowing that she was fervently opposed to feminism and women's empowerment, I was not surprised that she pressured me early to marry. Yet she and my father loved me and trusted my judgment. So it was with much ambivalence that she waved good-bye to me as I flew away that late August day in 1977.

"I arrived in the U.S. dodging marriage and pursuing an education. I saw myself as a sort of forced and yet chosen exile. While even here I was not fully immune to the global network of matchmakers, I was able to shrug them off with the buffer of time and distance.

"I began to explore the enticing dazzle of love and romance in the West. I observed people in and out of love and marriage; I examined the marvels of Cupid and Eros and wondered if I had been duped after all. I was stunned by the synonymous dimensions of love and lust in the West. For all the openness and accessibility in human interaction, facilitated by culture and technology, I found the extent of gender stratification in terms of ascribed and prescribed roles staggering. Conformity and convention were subtly but strictly assumed, and the rhetoric of 'freedom' was further perplexing, for in such a culture the individual was desolate and desiccated, *outside* community and hence needing to rush into relationships sexually and emotionally.

"The contrasts were compelling. In the East, I was struck by the primary identity of the individual as a member *of* the community, with attendant constraints. In the West, I saw individual license *apart* from community. Neither culture facilitated people to be *in* community and both seemed to prevent one's being fully human.

"Sea changes were taking place. The validity of marriage as a viable social institution had come under serious questioning, what with broken marriages, co-habitation, transient liaisons, the high costs of divorce, alimony, taxes and the general attack on traditional social arrangements. Marriages then are solely in the hands of the individuals involved and families take great pride in keeping their hands off their children's affairs. In the face of such shifting realities, I was forced to double-check my list.

"The love story writers of my youth had planted in me the perennial seeds of choice and possibilities, and my native culture had impressed upon me the significance of family and community support for blessed unions. Marriage in one system was assumed and therefore effortless and guaranteed. In the other, marriage lingered as a background reference. It was not guaranteed and hence took great effort, making people lonely schemers of one another.

"I was alone, once again, as I pondered these matters. What was I to do with a mottled life such as mine?

"I went home to India regularly. I was in constant touch with my parents and they pressured me to marry. I passed the cup on to God, all the while growing into a radical understanding of marriage and its place in this world. I had confidence in God's working. Besides, I was a happy and content single woman and I was strengthened by that.

"I continued to change. I was now ready to return to much of what I had left. *By golly. I too wanted an arranged marriage.* I wanted to marry a man who would be celebrated by kith and kin. There was something always right about a whole community saying 'We do' with you. There were other appeals to the arrangement by families: language, food habits, religion, class standing, etc. were shared by the two individuals. [For me there was] something more profound and precious: shared narrative. The recall of memory and the telling of stories are central to the survival of the human species from the local to the global level. One's sense of the past and present is crucial for one's movement into the future. The role marriage plays in this context cannot be overestimated.

"It became my opinion that elements of a traditional marriage although not sufficient were certainly preferable for the building of strong communities. I saw all around me the demise of marriages in the West. Any compelling reasons to stay committed to one another were increasingly few. The individual was all that mattered and the individual was frequently alone, rootless and rolling.

"In June 1990 I was en route to India. Was I about to surrender my present convictions and take on a new identity? In my new life I would have none of my old friends. Life would turn into a penance under my lord-husband and I would serve. I was to surrender and be subjugated to a man.

"I would be lying if I told you I had a quiet confidence in the knowledge of God's benevolence. Mine was a dejected surrender and emptying of myself to God in the face of uncertainty. I was weary after more than a decade of dilly-dallying with my parents on the matter of marriage. I realized it was still going to take a great deal of faith and trust in God and Life to say 'I do.' Now, I was taking my annual trip home to India. My parents had two-and-a-half men lined up for my interviewing. The third was only a half possibility. I consented to seeing all, even the unwilling half.

"On the way to Candidate #1, Abraham, my favorite code-words sounded powerful and tantalizing: 'turned-on,' 'chemistry,' 'madly in love.' But I was frustrated, for every single time I had met a potential mate, testing myself for these responses, I had been 'turned off.' So I approached Abraham almost perfunctorily, with fear and prayer.

"We spent two days in one another's company for about eleven hours in all, and left each other after postponing any major decision. I contemplated the one-and-a-half men left and was exhausted thinking about the ordeal. I hesitated to put them or myself through it. The most grueling part of these meetings is that you have to make up your mind in a matter of hours or less, and prepare to come with a press release explaining in detail why you have rejected him or her—the family must save face in the community. The reasoning has to be serious and concrete, e.g. 'ugly,' 'limps,' 'violent,' 'lecherous,' or 'mentally off,' not anything irrelevant such as views on politics, theology, feminism, human rights, poverty, or anything else.

"'What more do you want?' we were asked. 'He is educated, drawing a five figure salary.' 'She's so-and-so's daughter or niece.' 'He is the only son and sole inheritor.' 'She is strikingly beautiful,' we were told. My mother asked me, 'What is thirty or forty years in the larger scheme of eternity anyhow?,' referring to a potentially bad marriage and its insignificance. If you were to agree to the alliance—Hurrah! Ship ahoy and full steam ahead with plans for a gala celebration!

"Well, how did my time with Abraham go and why did we come to the conclusion we did? To put it bluntly, he did not 'turn me on.' Mind you, I didn't know what that meant except that my heart did not engage in somersaults while in his presence. I, of course, had been waiting for that to happen as a litmus test. He sensed my own reluctance, respected me, and left me with an escape hatch—'Go home and tell your folks that you need a little longer to think about it and by the time you break the bad news you will have returned to the U.S. and the blow won't be so hard to take.' The suggestion was a welcome relief. We agreed to write to each other over the next two months before we decided yea or nay. But it did not take me that long to be haunted by the Spirit of God.

"On the eight-hour train ride home I lay awake wrestling furiously with the idea of being 'turned on.' I took out my mental list of what I had been looking for, and to my consternation, I found that Abraham had showed me what I *should* be looking for. What do I mean?

1. He struck me as being honest and ordinary, qualities which I appreciated.
2. He did not play charades and force me to seek and find him. I suppose this is what my friends in the West are up against when they set out to 'know one another.'
3. The eldest of three, he had spent the last decade tending to his siblings after the death of their parents. This was the simple reason why he was still single.
4. He was a man with a quiet and deep sense of God's presence in this world and in his life. He was open to spending the rest of his life with himself. There was an Eastern sense of calm and contentment about him.
5. He did not take his achievements or his roots seriously (I gathered this from others).
6. In his marriage he wanted a woman with a mind and will of her own. He believed in encouraging her independence. He had a role model in his mother quite similar to my own.
7. He loved the world and was distressed at its sorrows.
8. As a physician he was more convinced than ever at the mysteries of God over against the masteries of men.

"I could go on. Suffice it to say that as the train ploughed through the black night across the sleeping Indian villages, in the quiet of my cabin I grew restless as I began to have an experience that is beyond explanation and understanding.

"I found myself gravitating helplessly back to Abraham. I had to embrace him in order to be complete. I thought of Ecclesiastes, 'a time to embrace.' Perhaps that time had come. I began to echo my mother's sentiments: What more do I want? Like a dog chasing his own tail, I went round and round trying to fix my need to be 'turned on' and shamefully I concluded that being 'turned on' was a dangerous hoax and it was a sure sign of ill health and danger. Stable and solid relationships were nurtured in the context of maturing love, not magical love that abandoned caution and wisdom.

"Dawn broke. Day came. I set my nocturnal ruminations aside. I wasn't about to concede anything to my eager parents. I needed time and distance for the decision. We had some unpleasant exchanges and I left for the U.S. three weeks later.

"October was the ultimatum Abraham and I had set to decide about our future. Even though much background research had been done for us, we felt the urgency of revealing to each other as much as we possibly could. It did not matter at all that we were not in one another's company as dating couples are. What was the point? Communication was all and this was optimally enhanced through letters and phone calls. I wondered if physical presence is more a hindrance in such situations, given the tendency to immerse one's self in the other's presence and person rather than to have healthy dialogues about things which matter. I am struck by the speedy involvement of physical bodies in the West, and the relative ease with which lust and dependency get misconstrued for love. Many a relationship founders because the *body* gets ahead of the *being*.

"I had been praying, and tried not to talk much about it to too many American friends for I knew no way of answering their question, 'But are you in love?' I didn't think they could understand. Our worlds and our paths were so different.

"And I was not in love.

"By September we sought one another's hand across the continents. In October, Abraham wrote asking if I wanted to substitute, in the wedding vows, 'to obey' with some sentiment more honest and realistic. I thanked him for the reminder, and chose to heed. By the end of December we were married in the cathedral where he had been worshipping. My friend Margaret stood by me as he tied the silken knot.

"Nearly five years have passed. I am still wondering what all those warnings meant: 'The first year will be the hardest.' 'Sometimes you will look at his face and wonder how you could have said Yes,' etc. Every day is one more in the story of love. Not long ago I asked Abraham how it was that two lives such as ours could be as miraculously and marvelously knit. His response was: the marriage was arranged long ago in heaven, it was merely celebrated by us mortals down below. I can't add to that. Our lives together are indeed all that the saints and troubadours announced and much, much more, by the mysterious grace and love of God.

"In this marriage I sense a divine blessing not only in our private lives but far beyond, in the larger world. The marriage has not taken away but has richly added to each of our lives in service to God and the world. In and beyond our daily sharing of food, language, faith, and culture is an ongoing covenant to preserve the common prayers and aspirations of our foremothers. While the specifics of our life experiences have varied, the major influences over the last three generations are the same in both our lives.

"Daily we embrace one another with a minimum of introductions and explanations, and that is gratifying. Silently nod together in reminiscences of the same stories back in India, many years ago, many thousands of miles and many peoples away. I wonder how much of the tragedy this world knows could be avoided by the bonds of love, ownership, and memory that couples, parents, children, and communities could have through the knowledge of interdependence and connectedness. Such ideas remain alien to those who look to be 'turned on,' and find themselves interminably dissatisfied.

"Marriage teaches me much. Most of all it teaches me about God's grace in Abraham's face."*

* Ivy George in *Perspectives* (Wenham, Mass.: Gordon College, January 1993).

Reflections on "An Arranged Marriage"

- As you compare the courtship methods of East and West, which seem to you most reasonable? most successful? why?
- What very different attitudes are reflected in those customs?
- Comment on Dr. George's statement that physical presence is often a hindrance to real communication.
- "Turned on"—a dangerous hoax?
- "There was something always right about a whole community saying 'We do' with you." Does that provide certain protections that we lack in America? If yes, enumerate.

34

Love and the Stranger

> From now on we regard no one from a worldly point of
> view. Though we once regarded Christ in this way, we do
> so no longer. Therefore, if anyone is in Christ, he is a new
> creation; the old has gone, the new has come!
>
> 2 Corinthians 5:16–17

John Vanderhorst is a minister, a technical writer, and the father of eight children. When he fell in love with Dotty he discovered that marriage to her would only come at a very high price. The world he had been living in, a "flimsy" one where he was always "hunting diversions," would be turned upside down, a prospect that gave him pause and a certain degree of terror. Here is his riveting account of that extravagant change.

"The obvious deduction, from the circumstances of our first times together, was that Dotty and I would physically consummate our love very soon. My own expectation was that sexuality would be a matter-of-course link between us from the outset. I thought this was to come quickly; I wondered how quickly. It was up to Dotty, and I didn't press her. I was quite comfortable waiting: it was good to be loved; it was good to be loving—to have that feeling of warmth and approval in my heart which I thought was love; and the anticipation of that finer and deeper intimacy to be accomplished through sexual union was a pleasure in itself—all of which gave me lots of patience. I even found pleasure in Dotty's reluctance, assuming as its cause a quaint coyness and laudable caution—it was only right that we knew one another a little before we made our bodies one.

"The disclosure of Dotty's virginity was one of the major surprises of my life. Here was a girl anything but frigid or fearful, and yet for obscure religious reasons she had disdained lovemaking. In unbelief I had to ask, 'Are you sure you've never . . . ?' She had not because she was a Christian. This news of course immediately altered my expectations for our relationship; what it did not alter was my desire to be with Dotty, to continue experiencing her love for me and mine for her. To these things I would desperately clutch—I thought they were salvation.

"What did it mean that Dotty was a Christian? To me it meant very little at first. It meant that we paused before meals to thank God for the food. And it meant that because we weren't married, we weren't to make love. Later it meant that because I wasn't a Christian, we weren't to be married; it was this finally which terrified me.

"To Dotty, being a Christian meant much more. I knew that by the way she talked of 'him'—Christ, the mysterious third party in what seemed a love triangle. As months passed, and his hold on Dotty did not falter, I wanted to say she'd abandoned me. I wanted to say that 'he' had diverted her love. I saw and felt the reverse. Her love for me was strong and real—somehow, I sensed, because of his hold on her. I was beginning to see that who Dotty was depended absolutely on what she believed—that the person she might have been, had she not known Christ, or the person she might become, should she repudiate him, would be a person very different from the Dotty I'd given my heart to. I didn't want her to change. I saw that 'he' would have to remain a part of the triangle.

"I thought I could live with that. I could share her with a stranger—if that meant she loved me the more. I hadn't reckoned, though, on how the Stranger would view things.

"I was told the Stranger (Dotty's friend) and I lived in separate worlds. It didn't need to be this way, and he didn't want it this way—I could choose in a moment to enter his world. Not to do so meant keeping the Stranger a stranger. I was satisfied with that footing, but in a way I hadn't yet grasped, it meant keeping the woman I loved a stranger as well. The alternative—to enter that other world—would require a step more daring and immense than I thought I could ever take.

"It was less easy now to look at the future squarely and not cringe. Before I had assumed simply that Dotty would not leave me. Of course she would need to adjust her beliefs a little, but our future together would survive. Now I saw it was no matter for her of 'adjusting beliefs.' We were living in separate worlds.

"Slowly I awakened to my own painful choice. Somehow a little romantic conflict had blown up into an ultimate cosmic question. I wanted the romance to be all; the stakes were simple and familiar. I wanted it to be her decision: 'Take me or leave me, as I am'; somehow she had thrust it back on me: 'I love you. Come and see his world.'

"The world I'd always lived in tended to be a flimsy one. For me it was a world of books and solitary walks and fantasies. It was where I was always hunting diversions. It was where I fled to the tavern to burrow in the crowd, yet couldn't forget my isolation. It was a world of catch-as-catch-can and look-out-for-yourself, for no one else would. It was not a glamorous world—though I always imagined that around the next bend it might become that way. It was not mostly beautiful—only at moments, which I consciously idealized as my framework for survival, I didn't love this world, but it was mine. I was attached to it. It was where I'd always lived—it was mine.

"I found myself in the stacks of Watson Library lifting from their shelves dormant volumes on the New Testament documents and the life of Jesus. I had agreed to investigate the Stranger's life and death. Actually I had mounted an attack. Pressured to enter peaceably into his world, I had slid from my inertia to begin a campaign of discrediting him, justifying my aloofness and preserving my own world. I was well-stocked with theories, arguments, challenges—the weapons with which I hoped to thwart his designs on my life. He was a distant, blurred figure, yet I rushed toward him and took aim.

"'The Stranger is a fiction,' I said. 'He's what men have dreamed up to treat perplexity.' 'He's their explanation for the inexplicable.' 'He's a superstition.' 'He's a personified ideology—just a way of thinking.' 'He's a hoax.'

"I thought of all the reasons why he couldn't be 'really there' the way Dotty said he was, and all the reasons why, even if he were, I could never know for sure. In the books I found sharper and more numerous weapons. Others before me had fought against him, even devoted their lives to the assault. They had left a stockpile of arguments I thought could not be withstood.

"Months later, lying on my back on my bed, I mused: 'Would I survive the afterthoughts, the aftermath—the first days or weeks with new pressures, new directions of thinking and believing, new people in very new ways, most of all him—all would enter and take control of my life, and would I survive? And the dangers, too, of intellectual afterthoughts. I would be in a new land without having much explored its resources, its way of life, its defenses . . . would I be safe? Would I remain as an inhabitant?'

"I was no longer the confident attacker digging up dead men's weapons to pit against The Stranger. I'd seen more clearly the further I advanced that the weapons themselves were old and dull. One by one, they had fallen harmless at the Stranger's feet. And my attack had brought me perilously close to him. Lying in the bare room, I sensed that just minutes remained in my old world.

"My heart raced. Defenseless, I turned a steady gaze upon him. He was near now, no longer so blurred. Faintly still—my eyes were adjusting—I saw a person 'really there.' I knew he had won. Of course he had never been in danger. He had taken an interest in my campaign, but from the start he had feared it only for its danger to me, not as any threat to himself. He was not gloating in his victory now; nor mocking the futility of my resistance. He longed for my surrender, not that he might punish me, but that I might find rest. He had felt my bitterness pass, and was waiting now for me to come.

"In the collapse of my mad campaign, so much had become clear. His world was for his friends, who loved him and sought his company. I understood I did not belong. I was a puny rebel, preposterously weak before his gentle might. Born in a world apart from him, I had ignored the signposts planted there to turn my steps toward him; every overture, every invitation, every warning I had ignored. First I'd thought simply to exclude him from my me-centered world. Later, in the panic of having to choose between my own world and his, I'd hoped to defeat him altogether. Through all this, he had waited. No, I did not belong in his world. Yet somehow he wanted to make me belong; he wanted me for his own.

"I understood now that my late foray against him had been part of a greater warfare—that I, and the men whose books had fueled my antagonism, were among myriads in a Resistance force opposed to him. It aimed, against his wishes, to keep him a stranger. Since an original revolt near the beginning of time, every man, every woman, had served in its ranks, on the front lines as fighters or as willing servants in an elaborate support system. Only by choosing to desert the Resistance and surrender to him could one meet him, know him, and enter his world. Oddly enough, when a Resistor did surrender, he was accepted, without reprisal, and welcomed like a brother by the one he'd opposed all his life.

"I understood he wanted to welcome me in just this way. Thinking I would have to let him, I turned once more to the scene of his triumph, centuries ago at a crossroads in time. He hung in pain beneath a furious, eclipse-blackened sky. His captors pricked and taunted him. Finally he died. The earth rumbled. He had finished his mission. He had, in yielding to the Resistance, permanently infiltrated its forces in a way to baffle its highest command. Its apparent victim, he had planned to lose. He had entered the Resistance world as a voluntary hostage to deliver men from its ranks. At his expense, any who might ever choose to change sides were free to do so. All were war criminals, but he had suffered their execution.

"He had suffered my execution. Now, master over death, he beckoned to me: 'Come.' It was a soft call. 'Come. Come, now.' I told him, 'Yes.' And a quiet knocking on my door roused me from the bed where, shivering and now soaring, I had surrendered my life to him.

"I realized, when I opened my door to Dotty, that she was now my second love."

Reflections on "Love and the Stranger"

- What *did* it mean, for John and Dotty's relationship, that she was a Christian?
- Is that Stranger's presence as unavoidably evident in our relationships as it was in theirs? Does He make a difference? If so, what kind?
- A genuine Christianity sharply clarifies alternatives. It is Christ or nothing—"an ultimate cosmic question."
- *Can* one enter peaceably into His world?
- Why do we so stubbornly resist surrender—even, at times, long after opening the door to Him?
- Why does He care to call us?

Conclusion

Is it possible to do the will of God in this day and age? It is possible to do the will of God in any age. Is it possible to buck the trends that come at us daily with such force? God is our Refuge and Strength.

This book does not offer a prescription for finding a life partner. Rather it presents descriptions of different ways in which God, our Guide and Guard, has worked with different people. There is no single formula for approaching marriage, but the recurrence of certain themes, methods, and timeless principles is noteworthy, for example the help of a third party in bringing together two people who were humble enough to listen.

It is encouraging to know that there are many men and women today who have given up dating altogether in order to avoid the minefield it seems to be. Confidently they have put their trust in God to bring them together with the one He alone knows is right.

I know one woman who has found it a good idea to limit dating solely to lunchtime. It's cheaper, briefer, and it's not dark!

I know another woman who, when asked for a date, told the man quite candidly that since she had reached thirty she was no longer in the dating scene but was ready for marriage. The man proposed shortly thereafter. A lesser man would have been scared off, which is probably just as well.

It would be a lovely thing if older people would do what was done in my mother's day. She met my father at a dinner party for young people, given by an older lady. Their courting was done in the safety of Mother's parlor at home. If they went out, it was with a chaperone or a group, never the two alone.

This collection of what might be called "cautionary tales" illustrates pitfalls to be avoided and principles to be adopted. A brief review of the latter may be helpful.

Aim, above all else, at *loving God*.

Make a wholehearted surrender of your life to God.

Believe that He takes you at your word.

Do not be surprised at the opposition of the adversary.

Pray, making your requests known to God.

Watch.

Expect Him to give you what He knows is best for you.

Receive His answer for today.

Trust His timing.

Obey God in the least thing shown.

Commit your uncertainties and fears to Him.

Act on principle, not on impulse; will, not emotion.

Accept the demands of your masculinity or femininity.

Remember that to take up the cross means suffering.

Do not walk into temptation. Flee.

Make a commitment to be not merely careful but *chaste*.

Keep your hands off and your clothes on.

Confide in and seek help from an older Christian.

Be grateful for your assigned portion (Ps. 16:5).

Praise and sing to the Lord. Thank Him for everything.

Keep a quiet heart.

Do the next thing.

Does the question "Will this work?" continue to trouble you, as though it were a mechanical contrivance that might malfunction? It is God we are dealing with, a just and merciful Father who is far more interested in our welfare than we are. Give the above list an honest try, in a daily time of silence and solitude. It might obviate dating altogether.

If one still feels that disciplined dating is permissible, may I hope that God's true gentlemen will have courage and forthrightness with the women to whom they are attracted. My father's rule for my brothers worked. Never mention love till you propose. Give yourself a time limit in which to make up your mind.

And a word for God's true women: Be feminine, be modest, be simple. Ask God for that gentle and quiet spirit that is a thing very precious in His sight. There is no need to flirt. The female of the species in the animal kingdom is clothed soberly. Keep your own counsel. There will be time enough to discuss feelings when the proposal comes. You will be glad you did not do the hunting.

> Find rest, O my soul, in God alone;
> my hope comes from him.
>
> Psalm 62:5

> O Christ, He is the fountain,
> The deep, sweet well of love!
> The springs of earth I've tasted
> More deep I'll drink above.
> There to an ocean fullness
> His mercy doth expand,
> And glory, glory dwelleth
> in Immanuel's land.
>
> Samuel Rutherford
> From "The Sands of Time"

If marriage is not in God's plan for you, may He give you grace to receive singleness as a gift to be embraced and offered back to Him with thanksgiving. Throughout Christian history single men and women have, by the living sacrifice of their aloneness, blessed the Church and found the fulfillment that spiritual parenthood offers. Rejoicing in the belief that the Lord has chosen them for a specially intimate relationship with Himself, they have brought forth fruit not only for time but for eternity. Their very "diminishment" has become their strength. Their quest for love has been transfigured into a glad self-offering, which is the deepest source of human happiness.

And now for you, my faithful readers, I give you this powerful promise that has carried me through many a bewilderment.

> Do not fear, for I am with you;
>   do not be dismayed, for I am your God.
> I will strengthen you and help you;
>   I will uphold you with my righteous hand.
>
> Isaiah 41:10

This is my prayer for each of you.

> May the God of peace make you holy through and through. May you be kept in soul and mind and body in spotless integrity until the coming of our Lord Jesus Christ. He who calls you is utterly faithful and he will finish what he has set out to do.
>
> 1 Thessalonians 5:23–24 *Phillips*

> Let us be Christ's men from head to foot, and give no chances to the flesh to have its fling.
>
> Romans 13:14 *Phillips*

Elisabeth Elliot is a popular seminar speaker, radio teacher, and best-selling author. Her books include *A Chance to Die, On Asking God Why, The Journals of Jim Elliot, The Mark of a Man,* and *Discipline: The Glad Surrender.*